AUTHENTIC
HOPE

AUTHENTIC HOPE

It's the End of the World as We Know It, but Soft Landings Are Possible

Jack Nelson-Pallmeyer

ORBIS BOOKS
Maryknoll, New York 10545

Founded in 1970, Orbis Books endeavors to publish works that enlighten the mind, nourish the spirit, and challenge the conscience. The publishing arm of the Maryknoll Fathers and Brothers, Orbis seeks to explore the global dimensions of the Christian faith and mission, to invite dialogue with diverse cultures and religious traditions, and to serve the cause of reconciliation and peace. The books published reflect the views of their authors and do not represent the official position of the Maryknoll Society. To learn more about Maryknoll and Orbis Books, please visit our website at .maryknollsociety.org.

Manufactured in the United States of America

Nelson-Pallmeyer, Jack.
    Authentic hope : it's the end of the world as we know it,
  but soft landings are possible / by Jack Nelson-Pallmeyer.
      p.   cm.
    Includes bibliographical references (p.   ) and index.
    ISBN 978-1-57075-957-4 (pbk.)
    EISBN 978-1-60833-116-1
    1. Social change – Religious aspects – Christianity.
  2. Christian sociology – United States. – I. Title.
  BR517.N45 2012
  303.49 – dc23   2011037237

To Sara

Contents

Chapter 3
Equity, Politics,
and the Common Good
53

Chapter 4
Good Riddance to Empire,
Part 1: Arrogance and Interests
81

Introduction

The world hasn't ended, but the world as we know it has—
even if we don't quite know it yet. —BILL MCKIBBEN[1]

It's the end of the world as we know it (and I feel fine).
—R.E.M.[2]

We can't know the content of a future that is yet to be lived, but many people sense, rightly I think, that the world and nation we've known are coming to an end. Present political, economic, ecological, and foreign policy problems are converging in ways that make it clear that the future will deviate significantly from what we have come to experience as normal. There are clear signs that we are entering a difficult transition period leading to an uncertain future that is likely to be very different from common expectations rooted in the recent past.

Bizarre weather events throughout the United States and much of the world have resulted in unprecedented heat waves, extended droughts, severe flooding, hurricanes, destructive tornadoes, famine, and rising food prices. These events verify deeper concerns expressed by scientists that the negative consequences of climate change are already present and that we will either act boldly to reduce greenhouse gas emissions or face a bleak future. As a leading U.S. climate scientist warns, "If human beings follow a business-as-usual course . . . life will survive, but it will do so on a transformed planet. For all foreseeable human generations, it will be a far more desolate world."[3]

Climate change concerns are not the principal sources of anxiety and uncertainty for most Americans. Millions of Americans are losing jobs, benefits, homes, and hope at the same time government services that might have cushioned these blows are being cut. The U.S. economy is in deep trouble, and there is little credible evidence that a lasting recovery is possible within the confines of traditional approaches. Debts, deficits, social cutbacks, a reckless and unaccountable financial sector, high unemployment, record home foreclosures, stagnant wages, expensive or unavailable health care, rising oil prices, threatened cuts to social security, deteriorating infrastructure, dysfunctional politics, disappearing safety nets, and the economic fallout from damaging weather events (climate changes) all contribute to anxieties that will deepen until we address structural problems. These include unprecedented levels of wealth and income inequality; ecological limits to growth; problems with oil use, supply, and dependency; the destructive political influence and priorities of moneyed interests and corporations; and the distorted priorities of a national security state that privilege expenditures for war and war preparation over other important needs.

The high human, social, and economic costs of war are other reasons for concern. The United States spends almost as much on its military sector as the rest of the world combined. Unprecedented military capabilities and global reach have long been viewed as visible expressions of U.S. power, but they are bringing about a rather speedy end to America's global dominance. As we will see, it was only a few years ago that American pundits and leaders spoke openly about empire and confidently about the effectiveness of U.S. military power to reshape the world. For many decades America's claim of moral, political, and economic superiority (American exceptionalism) was used to justify frequent wars, aggressive interventionism, and nearly unlimited military expenditures under the banner of national defense.

A culture receptive to militarization, war, and patriotism rooted in the idea of American exceptionalism is beginning to fray. Excessive military spending and interventionist foreign policies are making our nation less secure. They fuel international animosity and enormous budget deficits, cripple investments in essential infrastructure, and accelerate the pace of social, ecological, and economic decline. Unfortunately, the primary purpose of the Department of Defense isn't to defend America. As the conservative Cato Institute notes: "The United States does not have a defense budget. The adjective is wrong. Our military forces' size now has little to do with the requirements of protecting Americans." In fact our "global military activism wastes resources, drags us into others' conflicts, provokes animosity, drives rivals to arm, and encourages weapons proliferation. We can save great sums and improve national security by adopting a defense posture worthy of its name."[4]

Like it or not the U.S. global role will change significantly in years ahead (it is the end of the world as we know it). American militarism won't be tolerated by other nations. Also, the United States lacks the economic capacity or moral authority to continue aggressive, militarized policies. Whether the United States acts prudently to embrace a more modest foreign policy, reject militarization, and redirect resources to meet pressing needs remains to be seen. There are powerful groups resistant to change who benefit from excessive military spending and war, but soft landings are possible. There are many positive outcomes associated with the transition from militarized priorities to more modest foreign policies rooted in global partnerships. Our ability to be authentically secure as a nation depends on redirecting resources from war to solving pressing social, economic, and ecological problems. It is our responsibility as citizens and people of faith to work toward that end.

The dysfunctional state of U.S. politics adds to the anxieties felt by many Americans. Elected officials at all levels of government seem incapable of responding creatively and effectively to present challenges. Their diagnoses of problems and proposed solutions are often influenced or dominated by moneyed interests and corporations that prefer to stay on present pathways even if doing so undermines the common good and endangers the future. The problems we face are daunting but solvable. Solutions are possible but not within the parameters of present-day American politics. Elections don't have to be high-stakes auctions, and governance can be more than managing austerity.

LIFTING THE FOG

I write *Authentic Hope* in this context of deep and profound anxieties that envelope our nation like a thick, unwanted fog. I write because I see good reasons to be hopeful. As individuals and as a nation, we are living in a difficult transition period marked by disruption and discontinuity. The central premise of *Authentic Hope* is that we have an opportunity and a responsibility to shape the *quality* of our yet-to-be-determined future.

We are creative, resilient people. It is possible that we will see signs of crisis as opportunities and act accordingly. A collective awakening could allow us to change course, achieve soft landings, and enhance the quality of life even as we make profound changes in lifestyles, economies, foreign policies, priorities, and governance. Events five, ten, or thirty years from now can play out according to our better selves instead of our worst fears. This depends on our capacity to face problems honestly and courageously, envision and embody creative alternatives, and cultivate and sustain hope.

It is also possible, some would say likely, that the end of the world as we know it will be experienced as a series of unimaginable human tragedies. There are realistic scenarios in which the future is marked by nations struggling to deal with hundreds of millions of climate refugees and/or fighting a series of exhausting wars over shrinking supplies of oil, water, and other resources. There are already disturbing signs that U.S. military and civilian leaders are treating climate change as a *military* challenge and are preparing to wage an endless series of counterinsurgency wars. There is also much evidence to suggest that in the United States and elsewhere economic anxieties and fear provide fertile ground for mean-spirited politics. We cannot dismiss ugly scenarios because they are unpleasant. Neither should we see them as inevitable.

Authentic Hope explores values, visions, and practical pathways to a different but potentially better future. It highlights opportunities and possibilities while addressing four grave problems that may tempt us to despair: (1) climate change and ecologically destructive growth as the foundation of the economy, (2) massive inequality, (3) declining U.S. influence and power hastened by increased militarization; and, (4) dysfunctional corporate-driven politics. I write especially for people whose awareness of one or more of these daunting problems leads them to doubt their capacity to shape a positive future.

The good news is that when we act constructively to engage any one of these problems we create favorable conditions for resolving the others. Addressing climate change will require international cooperation and will be part of broader efforts to reposition economics within an ecologically responsible framework. Building an ecologically sensible economy will be conducive to peace because it requires greater equity and justice, and it reduces the likelihood of resource wars. Redirecting human and financial resources away from militarization and war will give us a realistic chance to deal with climate change and to enhance authentic security. Revitalizing politics and reigning in corporations will require a compelling vision of a good society, a fundamental reassessment of values and current priorities, and a vibrant social movement with sufficient power to demand and guide the multiple changes we need within the limited time frame we have for effective action.

DESCRIPTION OF CHAPTERS

Chapter 1, "Painful Positives: Moving Off Dead-End Roads to Authentic Hope," explores how finding solutions to current crises requires many changes and how abandoning dead-end roads is a key to authentic hope.

Chapter 2, "Ecological Economics: Healing Our Fragile Earth," examines alternatives to ecologically destructive growth as the foundation of the economy and the implications of climate change, including how we can act to minimize damages and maximize possibilities.

Chapter 3, "Equity, Politics, and the Common Good," examines present inequalities in the context of corporate-driven politics, and describes

Authentic Hope

many benefits of greater equality as we seek to improve quality of life and lessen ecological footprints.

Chapters 4,"Good Riddance to Empire, Part 1: Arrogance and Interests," and Chapter 5, "Good Riddance to Empire, Part 2: Possibilities," consider multiple ways in which declining U.S. influence and power are hastened by increased militarization and multiple benefits of choosing alternative foreign policies and pathways to security.

Chapter 6, "Values and Vision," posits that positive policy changes depend on better values. It describes ways of seeing the world that encourage transformational values that can guide our efforts to embody authentic hope, to respond effectively to pressing problems, and to build a sustainable future.

Finally, chapter 7, "Letters: Year 2055," looks at possibilities and consequences of the decisions we make during the critical decade of 2012–22.

As we seek to live responsibly in light of pressing problems and an uncertain future, it is important to keep in mind that we are not facing the end of the world. It's the end of the world *as we know it*. *Authentic Hope* is rooted in the premise that soft landings (meaningful alternatives) are possible. It is meant to encourage us to view serious problems through the lens of possibility and to choose authentic hope over inauthentic hope or cynicism. If we do so, then the quality of the future we shape may reflect our hopes more than our fears. No one can ask more of us, and it would be irresponsible to ask less of ourselves or others.

Chapter 1

Painful Positives:
Moving Off Dead-End Roads
to Authentic Hope

*Unless you change direction, you're apt to end up where
you're headed.* —CHINESE PROVERB

INTRODUCTION

When I speak about "the end of the world as we know it," I am not suggesting that we are fated to an apocalyptic end or some other national, international, or cosmic disaster. A high-quality future is possible if we abandon the dead-end roads on which we are traveling and if we embrace new pathways. When I speak about "dead-end roads" I mean to suggest that continuing to pursue policies and practices that cause serious problems won't lead to viable solutions. It is much more likely that staying on a problematic road will take us in the direction we are headed, which in the case of climate change, financial deregulation, economies divorced from equity and ecology, or aggressive wars, is over a cliff.

When I speak about "painful positives" I mean to suggest more than the fact that it isn't easy to discover that conventional wisdom may be wrong and that things we thought imminently reasonable turned out to be the source of major problems. I mean that we should be grateful for new knowledge that if taken seriously can prevent greater problems and open up possibilities for constructive change in the future. When I speak of "authentic hope" I mean hope we embody in all aspects of our lives

1

in response to problems we have examined honestly, courageously, and rigorously.

Think of the dead-end road on which an alcoholic travels. It is agonizing to watch the ever-expanding ripples of destruction that flow from the dysfunctional life of an alcoholic. It is exceedingly difficult for alcoholics to abandon the pathway they're on. It is also extremely difficult for a family to have the courage to arrange an intervention with a loved one addicted to alcohol or drugs. It is gut-wrenching for everyone involved, but an intervention is less painful than watching someone's addiction destroy that person, a family, and a broader circle of relationships. The intervention and subsequent counseling and treatments are painful positives because they open up possibilities for alternative futures. In a similar way, we face difficult choices when it comes to climate change, the economy, militarization, and politics: we can stand by and watch our nation travel on dead-end roads that lead over cliffs or we can make determined efforts to embrace alternative pathways.

DEAD-END ROADS: COMMON DYNAMICS

There are numerous examples of conventional wisdom encouraging dangerous travel on dead-end roads. I limit myself to one and draw conclusions about dynamics that are at play as we consider alternative pathways and deeper solutions to pressing problems involving climate change, ecologically irresponsible economics, militarization, and distorted politics. I've chosen industrial agriculture to illustrate a dead-end road that leads to the end of the world as we know it. The hi-tech, oil and chemical intensive agricultural system has achieved enormous productivity gains per input of labor and has provided many benefits to modern societies. It has also sown seeds of vulnerability. A story in the *New York Times* sheds light on why we will soon be forced onto alternative pathways: "Just as the heavy use of antibiotics contributed to the rise of drug-resistant supergerms, American farmers' near ubiquitous use of the weedkiller Roundup has led to the rapid growth of tenacious new super-weeds." Think of this dilemma as a simple equation:

Industrial agriculture's promotion of monocultures = Problems with weeds.

Problems with weeds = Use of Roundup to control weeds.

Use of Roundup to control weeds = Rise of superweeds.

Rise of superweeds = Need to reassess industrial agriculture.

The last equation, which includes reassessment, is reasonable but strongly resisted. The *New York Times* describes farmers caught on a treadmill as they seek to maintain high yields on superweed-infested, chemically dependent fields. To "fight" the superweeds "farmers through-out the East, Midwest and South are being forced to spray fields with more toxic herbicides." Farmers are beginning to question their reliance on monocultures and genetically modified corn, cotton, and soybeans, to which Roundup is applied in an unsuccessful attempt to thwart weeds. The rise of "superweeds could temper American agriculture's enthusi-asm for some genetically modified crops." A science policy analyst for the Center for Food Safety in Washington is quoted: "The biotech indus-try is taking us into a more pesticide-dependent agriculture when they've always promised, and we need to be going in, the opposite direction." Producers of Roundup and other chemicals have a different response. Roundup's failure, far from being a trigger to rethink assumptions, offers additional profit opportunities. Dow Chemical and other companies, the *New York Times* reports, are racing to develop more deadly herbicides and better genetically modified seeds that can resist them.[1]

This example of a dead-end road leading to "the end of the world as we know it" highlights four vital lessons to keep in mind as we seek to embody authentic hope and find solutions to pressing problems. First, it is hard to abandon well-established highways even if there is clear evidence that they are dead-end roads. Second, due to inertia and the interests of powerful corporations, proposed "solutions" often fail and cause further problems. The profit interests of companies make it difficult for them to acknowledge their role in causing the problems. The "solutions" they propose, therefore, are imprisoned within the confining logic of discredited roadways. We will see this dynamic at play whether the issue is health care reform, global warming, militarization and war, economic and tax policies, or regulating finance.

Third, like it or not, we will be forced off dead-end roads. The industrial agricultural system has dangerous flaws that will be impossible to ignore as superweeds and superpests proliferate, the quality of soil deteriorates, run-off from chemicals and animal wastes poisons water systems, oil supplies dwindle and costs rise, and as constraints linked to climate change and other ecological limits become clearer. Finally, the sooner we leave the dead-end road and embrace alternative pathways, the better our prospects for soft landings and the greater the likelihood that painful but necessary transitions will have positive outcomes.

GATEWAYS TO NEW POSSIBILITIES

The fact that we are being forced off familiar roadways (experiencing the end of the world as we know it) is good news even though it requires difficult adjustments. Staying on existing roads is the equivalent to driving willfully over a cliff. When we pay attention to the economic, ecological, and human consequences of climate change then both our generation and future generations won't have to deal with worst-case scenarios. When we stop attempting foolishly through militarism and war to secure oil and other resources, expand influence, dominate international affairs, or reduce terror then, we can enhance real security, diffuse anti-American hatred, and revitalize the U.S. economy. When we pursue alternatives to energy and resource-intensive economic growth, then we can reduce the

likelihood of resource wars and expand arenas for international cooperation. When we respect the ecological limits of a finite planet then we can
promote ecologically sustainable development, build green economies,
reenvision prosperity, and address pressing social problems. When we
offer compelling alternative visions and reign in corporate interests that
dominate politics and distort solutions, then we can reduce wealth and
income disparities, lessen poverty and social tensions, address social
problems, and enhance prospects for peace. We can revitalize democracy, unleash meaningful reforms, and overcome political cynicism with
a politics of hope.

Using present dead-end roads as pathways to building a hopeful
future is about as sensible as constructing new houses on quicksand.
Attempts to stay the course guarantee that problems will worsen. Being
forced off a dead-end road is a painful positive. It is disruptive, but it
opens up avenues to authentic hope. Leaving dead-end roads opens critical gateways to new possibilities. We may be able to achieve a "graceful
decline" in which the transition to a very different future improves the
quality of life for present and future generations.

AUTHENTIC HOPE

Addressing serious problems and repelling despair requires authentic
hope. The opposite of authentic hope isn't despair. It is inauthentic hope.
Inauthentic hope is optimism disconnected from reality.

- ◆ "We don't need to worry about climate change because it's a scam."

- ◆ "There's plenty of oil if we just get government regulators and environmentalists out of the way."

- ◆ "Bush ruined the country but Obama will fix it."

- ◆ "Obama and the Democrats ruined the country, but the Tea Party
  movement will fix it."

- ◆ "The United States is the greatest nation in the world and always will be."

- ◆ "They hate us because of our freedoms."

- ◆ "We'll be welcomed as liberators in Iraq."

- ◆ "We'll solve our problems in Afghanistan by escalating the war in Pakistan."

- ◆ "People who talk about ecological constraints to growth are like Chicken Little, part of a long line of discredited 'sky-is-falling' advocates."

- ◆ "We can meet our energy needs for centuries with clean coal and nuclear power."

- ◆ "Extending tax breaks to the wealthy creates jobs."

- ◆ "There are plenty of clean, alternative energy sources available so we can continue to grow the economy."

- ◆ "If we all switched our light bulbs and drove fuel-efficient cars we'd solve the problem of climate change."

At the heart of these and many other expressions of inauthentic hope is an irrational faith in our country's good intentions or in technology's ability to solve any and all problems. There is also the comforting illusion that solutions are possible without *us* having to do or change much of anything. Inauthentic hope is based on the promise that a bright future can be built on the foundations of present values, lifestyles, and national priorities. No fundamental reassessments or sacrifices are required. Like those whose plans for retirement involve winning the lottery, many people place their hope in fantasy solutions disconnected from reality.

HONESTY AND HOPE

Authentic hope pays attention to problems as they actually are to the best of our understanding, even if problems are grave and solutions are demanding or uncertain. As Rebecca Solnit writes:

> Unpredictability is grounds for hope, though please don't mistake hope for optimism. Optimism and pessimism are siblings in their certainty. They believe they know what will happen next, with one slight difference: optimists expect everything to turn out nicely without any effort being expended toward that goal. Pessimists assume that we're doomed and there's nothing to do about it except try to infect everyone else with despair while there's still time. Hope…is based on uncertainty, on the much more realistic premise that we don't know what will happen next.…When it comes to the worst we face, nature itself has resilience, surprises, and unpredictabilities. But the real territory for hope isn't nature; it's the possibilities we possess for acting, changing, mattering— including when it comes to nature.[2]

Soft landings in which present and future generations thrive are possible, but they hinge on our willingness to make profound personal, economic, and political changes. It is essential that we reject fantasy solutions and refuse to bury our heads in the sand. We need to overcome our reluctance to look at where dead-end roads are taking us. And we need to see clearly how staying on these roads prevents meaningful policy corrections and limits our life choices. Several factors feed our reluctance and cloud our vision.

Many of us who pay close or even partial attention to grave problems can easily feel overwhelmed. We may not be experts on economics or war or climate, but we know on some level that our nation isn't doing well and that local and global problems are getting worse. We fear that our lives and our nation may be headed over a cliff. Crashes aren't pretty, however, and so we turn away and push aside troubling thoughts.

Some of us are angry at the way things are and fearful about the future, but we pay little attention to the *causes* of serious problems. We are susceptible to hope peddlers who offer false and easy solutions or to fear peddlers who masterfully shift our gaze away from causes to other things. They provide us easy outlets for our anxiety and easy targets to scapegoat or to blame.

Another factor feeding our reluctance to face serious problems is that daily life and troubles are challenging enough. We worry rightfully about how to make ends meet. We fret about finding or keeping a job. We struggle to find affordable health care and housing. We worry about quality education for our children and wonder how to pay for college. We face many uncertainties as we approach retirement. Sufficiently pre-occupied, many of us minimize the seriousness of the threat or we trust naively that others, including business leaders and government officials, will find appropriate solutions without organized pressure to force them to do so. Our deepening insecurities are directly related to the troubling issues named above, but the immediate impact of experiencing greater stress and uncertainty in our daily lives is that we have less time, energy, or inclination to engage larger systemic problems.

Another obstacle to honest sight is our inability to see ourselves as agents and architects of meaningful change. We avoid looking closely at warning signs that pop up along dead-end roads because we are discouraged and don't see how to avoid the approaching cliff. Some of us are fearful, cynical, or nearly devoid of hope that things will ever change. Our challenge is to envision pathways to a fairer, more just, and more ecologically responsible economy, to see ourselves as actors capable of tackling problems and to take action because doing so is the right thing to do and because we believe it is possible that our efforts could enhance the quality of life for ourselves and future generations.

Although many of us benefit daily from the compassionate and caring actions of others and from the foundations of a caring society, we often view things more through the lens of fear than possibility. When we reverse this, our actions become living testimonies to possibilities rather than fears. Our lives and our communities are healthier. If we look carefully we can see how engaging problems and bringing compassion into public life gives our lives purpose and meaning. And we can see that such efforts are the key to building vibrant communities now and in the future. When we unlock our imaginations, we can see that rejecting American exceptionalism and pretenses to domination opens up pathways to authentic security. Embracing a more modest, less militaristic role for the United States in world affairs presents us with fantastic opportunities to shift resources and energy to address climate change, to build a better society, and to contribute to a more peaceful world. At present, however, it seems our imaginations are captive to fear. Not surprisingly, without compelling visions of alternative futures and of ourselves as key participants, we remain stuck on dead-end roads, reluctant to look honestly at where we are headed.

There are also cultural factors that feed our reluctance to face unpleasant realities. The allure and momentum of the consumer culture delivers novelty and temporary fulfillment along with a whole host of problems. Addictive consumerism drives the resource-intensive economy, discourages political engagement, and fuels debt and environmental degradation. It also fails ultimately to satisfy deep human desires for meaning and for purposeful living. Consumerism, even among those who seek "green" alternatives, can distract us and divert our gaze from problems that seem intractable, from possibilities beyond the reach of our imaginations, and from our responsibilities as citizens and people of faith.

Equally problematic on the cultural front is that we have internalized views and values that reinforce military priorities and war. The two dominant and defining features of American life today are national arrogance (hubris) and militarism. Arrogance is manifested in an exaggerated sense of national pride and an inflated sense of national purpose often referred to as American exceptionalism. Militarism finds expression in the inflated view of the usefulness of military power to provide security, defeat injustice, or promote goodness. Together American exceptionalism and militarism distort our sight and undermine our capacity for empathy and compassion. They discourage self-reflection and self-criticism. They prevent an honest reckoning of who we have become and where we are headed. They foreclose on any realistic possibility of transformation. Our cultural mindset turns U.S. soldiers into a strange hybrid of Rambo and Mother Teresa. As retired Lieutenant Colonel William J. Astore writes:

> We wage war because we think we're good at it—and because, at a gut level, we've come to believe that American wars can bring good to others (hence our feel-good names for them, like Operations Enduring Freedom and Iraqi Freedom). Most Americans are not only convinced we have the best troops, the best training, and the most advanced weapons, but also the purest motives. Unlike the bad guys and the barbarians out there in the global marketplace of death, our warriors and war fighters are seen as gift-givers and freedom-bringers, not as death-dealers and resource-exploiters. Our illusions about the military we "support" serve as catalyst for, and apology for, the persistent war-making we condone.[3]

There are additional problems on the cultural front that discourage an honest assessment of problems and solutions. Rooted in philosophical, religious, and secular belief systems, these cultural factors include many incompatible but widespread views. Some promote ideas concerning the inevitability of human progress and are susceptible to techno-fixes. Others stress the depravity of human nature, including original sin, and doubt our capacity to make necessary changes. Many religious systems understand human beings to be the pinnacle and ultimate purpose of creation with dire ecological consequences. Some pay little attention to social problems as they celebrate saviors and await second comings. And many religious systems have apocalyptic streams that abandon commitments to greater justice within history. They relish with great anticipation the actual end of the world, at which time God's vindicating violence is expected to reward them and other insiders while destroying their enemies.

Finally, our reluctance to truly face grave, life-threatening problems reflects an absence of authentic hope. To the degree that we recognize that problems are rooted in entrenched *systems* the more we feel the inadequacy of our *individual* responses. The vastness of the problems contrasts with our smallness. We feel insignificant in light of urgent needs that require profound changes. The refrain "I can't make a difference even if I want to" rings in our heads like an echo chamber. If it is true, and I believe it is, that hope requires honesty, then it is equally true that honesty requires hope. We are much more likely to face difficult problems and come to terms with the end of the world as we know it if we believe in the possibility of soft landings and that our political and life choices matter. All changes, big and small, depend on each of us choosing to live authentic lives. Hope is more than an idea we come to after weighing all the pros and cons. Hope is ultimately a choice we make that leads to action. To be authentic, hope must be embodied through creative, persistent engagement.

CONCLUSION

There is still time to embrace alternative pathways. A soft landing implies that it is possible for us to effectively address each of the monumental problems named above and arrive at places that offer meaningful life and hopeful prospects for present and future generations. When I speak about painful positives I express my belief that on the other side of facing difficult challenges is the possibility of a better future. Our nation can be better, more secure, a helpful global partner as we reject distorted visions of American global dominance and militarization and join the community of nations to address pressing problems. The steps we take to avoid the serious consequences of ecological neglect and global warming can enhance meaning and lead to healthier communities. There are alternatives to pillaging the earth to create jobs and many advantages to an equitable and sustainable economy. A people-centered, participatory democracy is both needed and possible. Social movements have succeeded in the past and have important roles to play in the present. When we choose wisely, when we reassess present values, lifestyles, priorities, and institutions, and when we advocate for immediate course corrections both big and small, we are *choosing* to sow seeds of hope. We are *choosing* to live authentic lives and to stake our hope in the possibility of a livable future. The prospect of achieving soft landings is enhanced greatly if we act boldly and soon.

Chapter 2

Ecological Economics:
Healing Our Fragile Earth

The question before us is not whether the natural disasters making headlines across the United States are somehow connected, but why we are so reluctant to connect them. My theory is that it's just too scary. If we admit that these extreme weather events have something to do with a global system, it feels too complicated to do anything about or prepare ourselves for. If we accept that climate change is something caused by the way we consume and produce everything from food to fuel, then we also have to admit that we need to fundamentally change the way our economy works. But no matter how daunting the challenge of climate change, we have to get our heads out of the sand. —JANET REDMAN[1]

Economic growth may be the world's secular religion, but . . . it is a god that is failing today—underperforming for most of the world's people and, for those of us in affluent societies, creating more problems than it is solving. It destroys the environment, fuels a ruthless international search for energy and other resources, and rests on a manufactured consumerism that is not meeting the deepest human needs. —JAMES GUSTAVE SPETH[2]

Prosperity speaks of the elimination of hunger and homelessness, an end to poverty and injustice, hopes for a secure and peaceful world. And this vision is important not just for altruistic reasons but often too as reassurance that our own lives are meaningful. It brings with it a comforting sense that things are getting better on the whole—rather than worse— if not always for us then at least for those who come after us. A better society for our children. A fairer world. A place where those less fortunate will one day thrive. If I cannot believe this prospect is possible, then what can I believe? What sense can I make of my own life?

—ECONOMIST TIM JACKSON[3]

INTRODUCTION

Economic and environmental bad news has dominated our lives the past several years and will likely do so until we abandon dead-end roads that divorce economics from ecology. The intersection of economics and ecology is the subject of the present chapter. I address what Tim Jackson, economics commissioner on Great Britain's Sustainable Development Commission, refers to as "the biggest dilemma of our times," namely, how we reconcile "our aspirations for the good life with the constraints of a finite planet."

We can no longer ignore the grave consequences of disconnecting economies and material aspirations from ecological sensibilities or stubbornly remain on dead-end roads marked by the relentless pursuit of growth. Authentic hope requires us to choose alternative pathways and redefine prosperity based on "a credible vision of what it means for human society to flourish in the context of ecological limits."[4] Our core challenge is to address climate change and build economies that reflect and respect the ecological systems that allow for meaningful life on earth. Meeting this challenge means reassessing the purpose of the economy, creating meaning-based societies, re-localizing ecologically responsible agricultural systems, creating alternatives to the consumer culture, focusing development on essential needs, and using fewer material resources to meet them. Soft landings are possible if we jettison economic theories and practices based on unlimited growth, build economies that promote equity and serve the common good (chapter 3) and reject militarized priorities in favor of meeting pressing needs (chapters 4 and 5).

WEATHERING THE ECONOMIC CRISIS

Economically and ecologically we are approaching the end of the world as we know it. The economic crisis known as the Great Recession was caused by Wall Street, but it shattered the lives of people on main streets throughout the country. The housing and financial crises that hit in 2007 and deepened in subsequent years were the result of a deregulation of finance that allowed and encouraged speculative investments without accountability. Millions of people lost homes, jobs, and hope. Retirement savings disappeared overnight. Unemployment skyrocketed and in 2011 25 million Americans were unable to find full-time work. Middle-class Americans scrambled to stay above water. Poor people with few assets were hurt most. Food insecurity, a situation in which household members have uncertain or limited access to enough food to lead an active and healthy life, increased significantly and impacted nearly one in four of America's children.[5]

As the economic and jobs crisis deepened, tax revenues decreased, and budget deficits increased. Public services were cut at a time when they were needed most. Many local, state, and federal government employees lost their jobs. Financially strapped consumers were unable or reluctant to spend given deep anxieties about the economy and their own futures. Many couldn't afford their prescriptions, lost health-care coverage along with their jobs, or dropped coverage because they couldn't afford the premiums. Corporations sat on a bundle of cash but were unwilling to invest or add jobs in an already depressed economy. If they invested they invested overseas. Rather than focus on the major causes of the economic crisis (chapter 3) politicians of both major political parties and the mainstream media focused a national conversation on debt and deficits. Predictably, government spending cuts during an economic crisis reinforced the economy's downward spiral.

The economy as presently structured doesn't deliver widely shared prosperity. Promises of a brighter future based on growth projections seem hollow. In this context it isn't surprising that many people ignored evidence of a deeper crisis in which the imperatives of an economy dependent on growth crashes against ecological constraints. If economic growth does return it is likely to be short-lived because of deepening environmental problems.

Visible signs that ecological problems would likely restrict economic growth included bizarre weather events linked to global warming and our economy's dependence on carbon-intensive fuels. Climate scientists are careful not to link any specific weather incident to global warming but they "can now make the statement that particular events would not have happened the same way without global warming," according to Kevin Trenberth, head of climate analysis at the National Center for Atmospheric Research.[6] The science is simple: Greenhouse gas emissions warm the planet and warm air holds more water vapor than cold air, which causes greater weather extremes.

Droughts, floods, and tornadoes ravaged many parts of the United States even as the Great Recession lingered. A *New York Times* article noted that during the first six months of 2011, forty thousand wildfires had scorched more than 5.8 million acres nationwide and warned that drought "could become a permanent condition in some regions." "In the South, 14 states are now baking in blast-furnace conditions—from Arizona, which is battling the largest wildfire in its history, to Florida, where fires have burned some 200,000 acres so far."[7] In Maryland 22 of 23 counties were declared natural disaster areas following a record-setting heat wave in 2010.[8] Texas withered under a summer of intense heat in 2011 as parts of the state experienced 100 degree temperatures consecutively for more than a month.

It is not only drought, heat waves, and wildfires that reveal harsh economic and ecological consequences linked to climate change. People in many parts of the country experienced other unprecedented and costly weather events. The U.S. Northeast experienced massive blizzards. The East Coast was battered by Hurricane Irene with Vermont experiencing its worst floods in a century. Floods in North Dakota, Minnesota, and Tennessee caused billions of dollars in damages. Alabama, Arkansas, Kansas, Massachusetts, Minnesota, and Missouri were hit with an unprecedented wave of tornadoes in 2011.

Damaging weather events are a common and costly worldwide phenomenon. In recent years, floods have ravaged Pakistan, Colombia, China, and Australia. Drought in Russia's wheat belt contributed to spiking food prices as a third of Russia's wheat crop was lost to scorching heat. Europe experienced a heat wave that killed thousands. In 2011, the Amazon experienced its second once-in-a hundred-year drought in the last five years. Extended drought in Somalia and Kenya triggered a humanitarian catastrophe. Ethiopia also grappled with its worst drought in sixty years.

DEEPER CRISES

Bizarre weather linked to climate change was only one manifestation of deeper ecological and economic crises. The global economy is driven by oil, and it is the burning of fossil fuels that drives climate change. As James Hansen and other climate scientists note:

> The science is clear. Human-made climate forcing agents, principally CO_2 from burning of fossil fuels, have driven planet Earth out of energy balance. . . . Global climate effects are already apparent. Arctic warm season sea ice has decreased more than 30 percent over the past few decades. Mountain glaciers are receding rapidly all over the world. The Greenland and Antarctic ice sheets are shedding mass at an accelerating rate. . . . Climate zones are shifting poleward. The subtropics are expanding. Climate extremes are increasing. Summer heat of a degree that occurred over only 2–3 percent of the globe, now occurs over 20–40 percent of Earth's surface each summer. . . . Global climate anomalies and climate impacts will continue to increase if fossil fuel use continues at

current levels or increases. Continuation of business-as-usual fossil fuel emissions for even a few decades would guarantee that global warming would pass well beyond the warmest interglacial periods in the past million years, implying transition to literally a different planet than the one that humanity has experienced. Today's young people and following generations would be faced with continuing climate change and climate impacts that would be out of their control.[9]

The production and use of oil is changing the planet. The BP oil spill in the deep waters of the Gulf of Mexico was the most costly environmental disaster in our nation's history. It also revealed that oil dependency is problematic in a world in which the easily accessible oil has already been tapped. Supplies are shrinking and more costly and dangerous to extract (this is also the case for many other non-renewable resources and minerals). Fighting wars for oil and energy in Iraq and Afghanistan (see chapters 4 and 5) didn't work out well either. Wealth squandered on wars hurt the U.S. economy and took much-needed funds away from efforts to transition to clean energy.

There is also an emerging pattern involving oil that reveals the limits to growth that go beyond problems of climate change and failed wars. When the U.S. and global economies experience robust growth, oil prices rise. Eventually rising oil prices hurt the economy and trigger an economic slowdown. An economic downturn pushes oil prices lower, which temporarily allows the economy to rebound. Each time the cycle repeats itself the starting point is more problematic because we are further along the dead-end roads of climate change and peak oil—the point at which present consumption outpaces current supplies and future oil discoveries so that each usage of oil amounts to a withdrawal from a limited and shrinking pool of oil.

ECOLOGICAL LITERACY

Present economic practices and presumptions of growth clash sharply with ecological imperatives. "Sustainability has had a hard time breaking into economic theory because the economics of the past fifty years has been overwhelmingly devoted to economic growth," economist Herman Daly writes.[10] Tim Jackson says bluntly: "Economics—macro-economics in particular—is ecologically illiterate."[11] Continuing on dead-end roads that ignore environmental constraints signifies willful ignorance. Abandoning them is difficult. Jackson, professor of sustainable development at the University of Surrey in Great Britain, names our dilemma clearly. To "resist growth is to risk economic and social collapse. To pursue it relentlessly is to endanger the ecosystems on which we depend for long-term survival."[12] Daly has argued for decades that in a finite world we need a steady-state rather than a growth-based economy. In a steady-state economy both population and overall resource use are stabilized within an ecologically sustainable framework.[13] Unfortunately, as Tim Jackson writes, the "capitalist model has no easy route to a steady state position. Its natural dynamics push it towards one of two states: expansion or collapse."[14]

The relentless pursuit of growth is a goal shared by communists and capitalists. It is promoted by most economists and nearly all politicians, peoples, and governments. Bill McKibben writes that in the United States the administrations that followed President Jimmy Carter had "a single-minded focus on economic expansion. The change was not just technological; it wasn't simply that we stopped investing in solar energy and let renewables languish. It's that we repudiated the idea of limits altogether—we laughed at the idea that there might be limits to growth."[15] Larry Summers, treasury secretary during the Clinton administration and President Barack Obama's chief economic advisor, said: We "cannot and will not accept any 'speed limit' on American economic growth. It is *the task* of economic policy to grow the economy as rapidly,

sustainably, and inclusively as possible."[16] "There are no . . . limits to the
carrying capacity of the earth that are likely to bind any time in the foreseeable future. There isn't a risk of an apocalypse due to global warming
or anything else. *The idea that we should put limits on growth because of
some natural limit is a profound error."*[17] When Herman Daly asked him
what the "optimal scale" of the macro economy was "relative to the environment" Summers responded: "That's not the right way to look at it."[18]

Daly says traditional economics ignores the "simple and obvious"
fact that economies "are increasingly constrained by the depletion and
pollution of a finite environment." This omission discredits much of
what passes for economic orthodoxy which "explains why it cannot be
contemplated by the growth economists."[19] As McKibben notes, "every
force in our society is trained to want more growth. . . . The way our
economy works at present, any cessation of growth equals misery."[20] No
wonder few people seriously question the link between prosperity and
growth. The troubling consequences of this pursuit are resource wars and
environmental collapse accompanied by economic and social trauma.
"We know from earlier civilizations," Lester Brown writes, "that the lead
indicators of economic decline were environmental, not economic."[21]

TEMPTING ILLUSIONS

We live with the tempting illusion that economies, population, agriculture, energy use, and lifestyles can grow or function independent of
ecological constraints. "Civilization has been . . . slow to give up on
our myth of the Earth's infinite generosity," Barbara Kingsolver writes.
"Declining to look for evidence to the contrary, we just knew it was
there. . . . Rather grandly we have overdrawn our accounts."[22] One measure of ecological overdraft is going into the "ecological red," the point
each year when our economic footprint exceeds the earth's environmental resource budget. It takes the earth about eighteen months to generate
what we consume in just twelve.[23] The earth's ecological systems are

already assaulted by the demands of present human numbers and levels of consumption. Meanwhile, global population is expected to rise from 7 billion in 2011 to 9 billion by 2050, and many people will seek greater material affluence.

Economists express faith that growth projections can be achieved by efficiency gains that reduce the ecological intensity of each unit of economic output, a process known as decoupling. But as Jackson notes: "Nowhere is there any evidence that efficiency can outrun—and continue to outrun—scale in the way it must do if growth is to be compatible with sustainability."[24] History, he says, "provides little support for the plausibility of decoupling as a sufficient solution to the dilemma of growth." In fact, global "resource intensities (the ratio of resource use to GDP), far from declining, have increased significantly across a broad range of non-fuel minerals. Resource efficiency is going in the wrong direction." Efficiency gains have not "even compensated for growth in population, let alone the growth in incomes."[25] The "notion that we can save the 'growth forever' paradigm by dematerializing the economy, or 'decoupling' it from resources, or substituting information for resources, is fantasy," Daly writes. "We can surely eat lower on the food chain, but we cannot eat recipes!"[26]

A corollary to the theme of salvation through greater efficiency is the idea that technology will save us. Technology is purported to overcome environmental limits to growth and remove risk from everything from nuclear power to speculative finance. "If there is one true religion in the US, it leads us to worship at the altar of technology," Anne and Catherine Lutz write. "Christian or Jew, Muslim or atheist, we accept the doctrine of this shared faith: that technology provides the main path to improving our lives and that if it occasionally fails, even catastrophically, it will just take another technology to make it all better."[27] "Experts in both the nuclear and finance industries assured us that new technology had all but eliminated the risk of catastrophe," Joseph Stiglitz writes. "Events proved them wrong: not only did the risks exist, but their consequences were so enormous that they easily erased all the supposed benefits of the systems that industry leaders promoted."[28]

Value-driven technology that meets essential needs within the boundaries of ecological limits and social justice will be a vital part of the transition to a sustainable world. Unfortunately, many technological developments aggravate rather than solve environmental problems. The overwhelming priority for U.S. federal research and development funding is how better to kill people and wage future wars.[29] Many new commercial technologies don't help either. They often result in slight improvements to an existing product line. The result, with a boost from advertisers, is a buy-discard-buy cycle as people purchase the latest version of a product. This is good for growth and bad for the environment. The improved product *may* be produced with fewer inputs or resources per unit of production. Effective advertising and global markets, however, result in increased sales so that ecological impacts rise substantially because the scale of total sales and resource use outpaces efficiency gains.

Many technological advances encourage the relentless pursuit of growth with dire ecological consequences. As Daly notes, "By now it should be clear that not every new technology that comes down the pike is a net benefit to the human race. . . . We need technologies of development, not technologies of growth . . . [that have] larger jaws and a bigger digestive tract."[30] Examples abound of technologies that keep us on dead-end roads. Production of ethanol and biofuels from corn, soy and, palm oil aggravates many problems from water pollution to world hunger. Companies tap oil miles below the ocean's surface but, as the BP oil spill demonstrates, doing so carries potentially catastrophic risks. Technology makes it possible to produce oil from tar sands and shale, but if much of this oil is extracted and used (Canadian tar sands hold the world's second largest deposits of oil estimated at 300 billion barrels) there will be no chance of preventing runaway climate change.[31]

Similarly, a new generation of nuclear plants utilizing better technology and standard designs is supposed to make nuclear power safe and efficient, but to generate electricity with nuclear power is perilous. In March 2011 an earthquake and tsunami devastated Japan and overwhelmed and obliterated all systems meant to safeguard its nuclear power plants. As the nuclear crisis deepened and the threat escalated, a stream of U.S. experts and politicians defended nuclear power, which was said to be essential, safe, and clean! The *Minneapolis Star Tribune* reported that the "Obama administration will apply lessons learned from Japan's catastrophic nuclear accident but will continue to speed reactor construction." President Obama "would not back away from his commitment to expand nuclear generation of electricity" in order to address climate change and reach his goal "to generate 80 percent of the nation's electricity from *clean* sources by 2035."[32]

I'm not sure which is more startling: designating an energy source "clean" that generates waste that is deadly for half a million years or a false confidence in technology that reflects hubris bordering on idolatry. Amory Lovins, in the aftermath of the catastrophe in Japan, wrote: "Each dollar spent on a new reactor buys about two to ten times less carbon savings, and is 20–40 times slower, than spending that dollar on the cheaper, faster, safer solutions that make nuclear power unnecessary and uneconomic: efficient use of electricity, making heat and power together in factories or buildings ('cogeneration'), and renewable energy."[33]

In sum, we are foolish to project technologies that keep us on dead-end roads as means to salvation. Many new technologies extend the life of dead-end roads, aggravate pollution problems, and increase the likelihood of catastrophic accidents, spills, and climate change. The end point of dead-end roads is clear. Population growth and greater resource use on a finite planet push us into the ecological red earlier each year. Eventually, the resulting environmental crises will reduce human numbers, affluence, and arrogance. This is not our fate, but it is where we are headed.

SEDUCTIVE AND CONVENIENT
GROWTH SCENARIOS

The idea that the economy can grow indefinitely allows us to ignore limits and enables the economically powerful to deflect attention away from pressing needs for greater justice, equity, and sustainability. Economic growth is clearly an inadequate means to end poverty. In the United States one in five children lives in poverty and the richest four hundred Americans have more cash and assets than the combined total of 150 million Americans.[34] After decades of growth in world trade and the global economy, nearly half the world's people are struggling to survive on less than $2.50 a day while the three richest people have assets greater than the combined gross domestic products (GDPs) of the poorest forty-eight countries. The poorest 1.25 billion people receive about 1.1 percent of the world's total income and the richest 20 percent of the global population consumes about 86 percent of the world's resources. "The political difficulty of facing up to sharing, population control, and qualitative development as the real cures to poverty will sorely tempt politicians to resurrect the impossible goal of growth," Daly writes, "more for all with sacrifice by none, forever and ever, world without end, amen. . . . No doubt they will want to call it 'sustainable growth.'"[35]

Soft landings require more equity and greater justice (chapter 3). When the U.S. economy grows or if promises of future growth seem believable, however, many people accept arguments that there are no natural limits to growth and no need to reassess basic fairness. Everyone is presumed to benefit from a bigger pie. Growth trumps the environment, equity, and justice. As President Barack Obama said in response to a question about poverty, "I think the history of anti-poverty efforts is that the most important anti-poverty effort is growing the economy. It's more important than any program we could set up. It's more important than any transfer payment we could have."[36]

A growing economy is supposed to make us all richer, help the poor, and pay for a cleaner environment. This isn't the case when the benefits of economic growth are concentrated in the hands of the wealthy few (chapter 3). An additional problem is that economists measure growth by calculating GDP, a poor measure of personal, social, or ecological well-being. GDP measures a nation's total spending by government, households, and investors. It doesn't account for non-market services, for inequality, or for depletion of ecological assets that limit future consumption. In economic terms, pollution is a positive. "No attention is paid by the GDP . . . to the health or environmental costs of pollution or the depletion of natural resources," Jackson writes. "By contrast, all kinds of things are included in the GDP—the costs of congestion, oil spills, and clearing up after car accidents." Counting these "as contributing meaningfully to economic welfare seems perverse."[37] "The richer we get, the poorer we become ecologically and culturally," Vandana Shiva writes. "The growth of affluence measured in money, is leading to a growth in poverty at the material, cultural, ecological and spiritual levels."[38]

By projecting growth indefinitely into the future we postpone difficult choices. We avoid troubling conversations about the costs and consequences of mindless consumption, saddling future generations with massive financial and ecological debts and rapid population growth. Future economic growth will compensate for today's excessive consumption paid for with borrowed money, the argument goes. If economic growth rates exceed birth rates then thorny issues like limiting human numbers can be avoided. Lester Brown points out troubling shortcomings of this argument: "Each year there are 79 million more people at the dinner table. Unfortunately, the overwhelming majority of these individuals are being added in countries where soils are eroding, water tables are falling, and irrigation wells are going dry," Brown writes. "If we cannot get the brakes on population growth, we may not be able to eradicate hunger."[39]

To set limits of any kind is seen as limiting human freedom. But as Jackson notes, "there is an irredeemably moral dimension to the good life." "In a world of limits, certain kinds of freedoms are either impossible

or immoral. The freedom to accumulate material goods is one of them."
The freedom "to find meaningful work at the expense of a collapse of
biodiversity or to participate in the life of the community at the expense
of future generations may be others."[40] The freedom to procreate at the
expense of other species is another.

IRRESPONSIBLE AND DANGEROUS GROWTH SCENARIOS

The promise of unlimited growth "demonstrates a long-term blindness
to the limitations of the natural world."[41] Today's signs of ecological
stress are fruits of past and present growth policies. Biologists at the
United Nations Convention on Biological Diversity estimate that species are disappearing up to a thousand times faster than the natural rate
of wildlife loss. "This is due to habitat destruction; expansion of agriculture; deforestation; overexploitation of biological resources such as
fish; invasive species; and, on top of that, climate change."[42] Scientists
report in the journal *Nature* that rivers serving 80 percent of the world's
population are so badly impacted by human footprints that the survival
of thousands of aquatic species, and the water security of nearly 5 billion people, are threatened. "Our study found that vast areas across both
the developed and developing world arrive at similarly acute levels of
imposed threat to their freshwater resources."[43]

Many of the world's freshwater aquifers are being mined in excess of
replenishment rates. Water tables are "now falling in almost every country
that irrigates with underground water," and many of these countries "are
facing hunger-inducing losses of irrigation water as aquifers are depleted
and wells go dry," Lester Brown writes. "Both soil erosion and aquifer
depletion reflect an emphasis on current consumption at the expense of the
next generation."[44] Brown describes troubling trends in China:

> Since 1950, some 24,000 villages in the northwestern part of the
> country have been totally abandoned as sand dunes encroach on

cropland. And with millions of Chinese farmers drilling wells to expand their harvests, water tables are falling under much of the North China Plain, which produces half of the nation's wheat and a third of its corn. Chinese agriculture is also losing irrigation water to cities and factories.[45]

Worldwide people are robbing the future to enable present excess amid profound inequalities. This is also the case with water intensive energy production involving coal, oil from shale or tar sands, natural gas production using a method known as fracking, and nuclear power. All use and contaminate huge quantities of fresh water.[46] "It is not just that energy production could not occur without using vast amounts of water. It's also that it's occurring in the era of climate change, population growth, and steadily increasing demand for energy," Keith Schneider notes. "The result is that the competition for water at every stage of the mining, processing, production, shipping, and use of energy is growing fiercer, more complex and much more difficult to resolve."[47] Peter Gleick, a water expert and president of the Pacific Institute in Oakland, says: "We're going to see rising tensions over shared water resources, including political disputes between farmers, between farmers and cities, and between human and ecological demands for water. And I believe more of these tensions will lead to violence."[48]

Unmet water and sanitation needs already undermine quality of life for many of the world's people. Women in the developing world walk on average 3.7 miles daily in search of water.[49] The United Nations estimates that between 800 and 900 million people lack access to safe drinking water and more than 2.6 billion people have no access to basic sanitation.[50] As Maude Barlow of the Canada-based Blue Planet Project says: "No clean water, no food; no clean water, no health; no clean water, no schools; no clean water, no equality of rights; no clean water, no peace."[51]

Climate changes are impacting water quality in a variety of ways, all negative. The ocean is losing its capacity to absorb CO_2, and present concentrations have led to acidification that threatens the ocean food chain. Warmer temperatures are increasing the rate and intensity of floods, droughts, and heat waves. This translates into serious hunger concerns as crops wither and crop land is destroyed. When it comes to global warming small numbers have big implications. Barbara Kingsolver notes that we've raised the earth's temperature by .7 degrees Celsius (1.3 degrees Fahrenheit). This is "a number that seems inconsequential. But these words do not: flood, drought, hurricane, rising sea levels, bursting levees."[52] Similarly, CO_2, emissions are rising about 2 parts per million (ppm) a year. This doesn't sound alarming, but for thousands of years leading up to the carbon-intensive industrial revolution, the earth's atmosphere had stable concentrations of CO_2 at about 275 ppm. By 2011 they had reached 390 ppm. Many scientists now believe the safe level of carbon in the atmosphere to be 350 ppm.[53] Adding 2 ppm of carbon to the atmosphere each year increases carbon concentrations at ten thousand times the normal rate![54] "Our children, grandchildren, and many more generations will bear the consequences of choices that we make in the next few years," James Hansen writes.[55] "It's not too late. [A positive] outcome is still feasible in the case of global warming, but just barely."[56]

One sign of global warming is that land-based glaciers are in retreat almost everywhere,[57] including in Asia, where they provide water for more than 2 billion people. The short-term impact of glacier retreat and melt is too much water. The long-term consequence is not enough. "This situation—too much water, too little water—captures, in miniature, the trajectory of the overall crisis," Brook Larmer writes in *National Geographic*. "Even if melting glaciers provide an abundance of water in the short run, they portend a frightening endgame: the eventual depletion of Asia's greatest rivers. . . . Along with acute water and electricity shortages, experts predict a plunge in food production, widespread migration in the face of ecological changes, even conflicts between Asian powers."[58]

Growing competition over food and land use has enormous social and environmental implications. In 2008 food riots broke out in thirty countries as prices for basic grains and foods skyrocketed. Many factors contributed to the price rises, including reduced harvest due to poor weather, rising oil prices, market speculation, increased consumption of meat in countries such as India and China, and "the massive use of grain to fuel cars."[59] Prices spiked again in 2011. "Each year, the world demands more grain, and this year the world's farms will not produce it," writes Tim Searchinger in a *Washington Post* article: "How Biofuels Contribute to the Food Crisis." "World food prices have surged above the food crisis levels of 2008. Millions more people will be malnourished, and hundreds of millions who are already hungry will eat less or give up other necessities. Food riots have started again."[60] Lester Brown writes that "food has quickly become the hidden driver of world politics."[61] Writer Christian Parenti notes that uprisings in Kyrgyzstan, Kenya, Libya, Yemen, Syria, and Egypt between June 2010 and June 2011 were all linked to rising grain prices. He refers to them as "bread-triggered upheavals."[62]

Biofuels drive price increases and shortages, Searchinger writes, because demand "for biofuels is almost doubling the challenge of producing more food." Since 2004, "for every additional ton of grain needed to feed a growing world population, rising government requirements for ethanol from grain have demanded a matching ton. Brazil's reliance on sugar ethanol and Europe's on biodiesel have comparably increased growth rates in the demand for sugar and driven up demand for vegetable oil."[63] In America, 40 percent of the corn crop, nearly 5 billion bushels, is currently diverted to make fuel for cars.[64]

Producing food to feed people in a sustainable way is possible with the right values and policies (see below). But when you produce food for fuel and define hunger solutions in terms of more high-tech production and not greater equity and justice, you further expose the limitations of industrial agriculture and exacerbate ecological and social problems. European demand for biofuels has dramatically increased CO_2 emissions as tropical forests are cut to make way for palm oil. Similarly, corn-based ethanol causes more CO_2 emissions if you factor in land-use changes elsewhere as forests and uncultivated lands are cleared for food production in an attempt to make up for losses attributed to the use of food for fuel. Corn-based ethanol has other serious drawbacks, described by Carolyn Lochhead in the *San Francisco Chronicle*:

> Each year, nitrogen fertilizer used to fertilize corn, about a third of which is made into ethanol, leaches from Midwest croplands into the Mississippi River and out into the gulf, where the fertilizer feeds giant algae blooms. As the algae dies, it settles to the ocean floor and decays, consuming oxygen and suffocating marine life . . . The gulf dead zone is the second-largest in the world . . . Scientists say the biggest culprit is industrial-scale corn production. Corn growers are heavy users of both nitrogen and pesticides. Vast monocultures of corn and soybeans, both subsidized by the federal government, have displaced diversified farms and grasslands throughout the Mississippi Basin.[65]

Intensive production of corn also aggravates soil erosion and displaces wildlife habitat. Although soil erosion has been reduced on U.S. farms since 1982, according to the 2007 National Resource Inventory (NRI) produced by the USDA's National Resources Conservation Service, the average Iowa farm loses five tons of top soil per acre each year.[66] According to the National Wildlife Federation, increased ethanol production has meant planting corn on thousands of acres of pristine wildlife habitat. "Our research shows that native grassland is being converted into cropland at an alarming rate. . . . As a result, populations of sensitive wildlife species are declining significantly in areas with high increases in corn plantings."[67]

Diverting food crops to fuel also creates tight markets that allow speculators to create and profit from human misery. According to twenty-five-year trader Daniel Dicker, financial traders using investment vehicles that didn't even exist a few years ago "capitalize on the supply shortages" and cause market imbalances that contribute to food bubbles.[68] Mariann Bassey, African food and agriculture coordinator for Environmental Rights/Friends of the Earth Nigeria, describes the impact of speculative investment in relation to biofuels:

Rural communities and the environment in poor countries are being ignored in the rush for our land and resources. This is a problem that has been created by rich nations and is being pursued with relentless speed by overseas companies across the global south. The world has got to say stop to land grabbing. A clear cause of land grabs is the demand for biofuels. This demand is transforming our natural resources into fuel crops, taking away food-growing farmland, and creating conflicts with local people over land ownership. We are suffering just so that Europe and developed nations can fuel their cars and lorries.[69]

Another damaging response to the 2008 food crisis is that foreign investors and speculators have targeted the agricultural land of poor countries with serious hunger problems for development of export agriculture. John Vidal in an article titled "How Food and Water are Driving a 21st century African Land Grab," notes that Ethiopia, "one of the hungriest countries in the world," is offering up millions of hectares "of its most fertile land to rich countries and some of the world's most wealthy individuals to export food for their own populations." It is one of twenty or more African countries "where land is being bought or leased for intensive agriculture on an immense scale in what may be the greatest change of ownership since the colonial era." Vidal notes that the land rush has been triggered by worldwide food and water shortages and the European Union's biofuels mandate. "In many areas the deals have led to evictions, civil unrest, and complaints of 'land grabbing.'" Leading the rush, he notes, "are international agribusinesses, investment banks, hedge funds, commodity traders, sovereign wealth funds as well as UK pension funds, foundations and individuals attracted by some of the world's cheapest land."[70] Groups such as La Via Campesina, Food First Information and Action Network (FIAN), and the Land Research Action Network have denounced World Bank complicity in land grabbing schemes in rural communities across Africa, Asia, and Latin America. These groups note that World Bank proposals and corporate investors "distract from the fact that today's global food crisis will not be solved by large-scale industrial agriculture, which is what all of these land acquisitions are about."[71]

Damaging competition between food for fuel, and food for local consumption versus food for export offers further evidence that growth scenarios fail to respect ecological limits or the needs of the poor. There are other troubling signs that the industrial agricultural model is a dead-end road. Run-off of pesticides, herbicides, and nitrogen pollute America's rivers and contaminate wells. "Here in the heart of southeast Minnesota farm country, everyone knows you don't drink the water," Josephine Marcotty writes in a February 2011 article in the *Minneapolis Star Tribune*. "It's just not safe," farmer Linda Liebfried says. "Every doctor will say not to drink it." "Minnesota cannot take the next step in preserving its lakes and rivers without addressing one of the last, biggest sources of pollution: agriculture," Marcotty writes. Forty percent of the "state's lakes and rivers are impaired, and with nearly half of the state's land mass devoted to crops, the vast amount of chemical runoff that comes from agriculture is a major factor."[72]

Industrial agriculture's approach to animal production also causes serious problems. Confining animals in feedlots concentrates waste and contributes to global warming. The livestock sector accounts for about 9 percent of CO_2 emissions but is responsible for a much higher percentage of other, more intense greenhouse gases, including 37 percent of methane and 65 percent of nitrous oxide emissions.[73] Concentrated animal production and waste also threaten water supplies and lead to serious abuse of drugs. The Food and Drug Administration reported that 29 million pounds of antimicrobial drugs were sold for therapeutic and nontherapeutic use for farm animals in 2009.[74] Margaret Mellon, director of the Union of Concerned Scientists Food and Environmental Program, says: "Antimicrobial use in U.S. animal agriculture is way out of proportion of what is necessary. And that poses dire risks for human health by undermining the effectiveness of these drugs."[75] "You can pass all the laws you want, organize all the boycotts," author David Kirby writes. "But ultimately when you cram thousands of animals into a single confined space without access to fresh air, outdoor sunlight, pasture, natural animal behaviors—you are asking for problems in the form of diseases that attack people." Some solutions include: ban nontherapeutic use of antibiotics in animals; break up processing monopolies; cut billions from agribusiness subsidies; and support small independent farmers.[76]

Past and present growth practices have resulted in serious ecological debts that must be paid. Seeking "solutions" on the dead-end road of growth is dangerous and irresponsible. "On our new planet growth may be the one big habit we finally must break," Bill McKibben writes.[77] A true measure of ecological debt factors in the environmental consequences of using renewable resources at unsustainable rates and the mining, depletion, use, and discard of nonrenewable resources and products that contribute to serious ecological problems such as climate change and pollution of land, water, and air. Banks impose stiff penalties when spending exceeds our bank balance. Nature does too. Lester Brown writes:

> We are consuming renewable resources faster than they can regenerate. Forests are shrinking, grasslands are deteriorating, water tables are falling, fisheries are collapsing, and soils are eroding. We are using up oil at a pace that leaves little time to plan beyond peak oil. And we are discharging greenhouse gases into the atmosphere faster than nature can absorb them, setting the stage for a rise in the earth's temperature well above any since agriculture began. . . . In addition to shrinking forests and eroding soils, we

must deal with falling water tables, more frequent crop-withering heat waves, collapsing fisheries, expanding deserts, deteriorating rangelands, dying coral reefs, melting glaciers, rising seas, more powerful storms, disappearing species, and, soon, shrinking oil supplies.[78]

ABSURD GROWTH SCENARIOS

Today's misuse of renewable resources and rapid depletion of non-renewable resources damage the environment and threaten present and future generations. Projecting future growth involving greater abuse and misuse of resources as the basis of future prosperity is absurd. "We may not yet know exactly where all the limits lie. *But we know enough to be absolutely sure that, in most cases, even the current level of economic activity* is destroying ecological integrity and threatening ecosystem functioning, perhaps irreversibly," Jackson writes. "To ignore these natural bounds to flourishing is to condemn our descendents—and our fellow creatures—to an impoverished planet."[79]

China today consumes more basic resources than the United States, including more coal and grain, three times more steel, and nearly twice as much meat. Although China lags well behind the United States in per capita consumption of these basic resources and the United States has a wide lead in total oil consumption, the gaps are likely to narrow. Under present growth scenarios, per person consumption in China would reach present U.S. levels in 2030. China would then use twice as much paper as the world presently produces. If it emulates U.S. car use China would consume 98 million barrels of oil a day, 13 million barrels more than current total daily oil production! Of course we also have to factor in the United States, India, Brazil, and every other country in the world. It is ridiculous to project growth of this kind on a finite planet that is already approaching peak oil and experiencing serious environmental stresses. As Jackson notes:

Economic expansion in China and the emerging economies has accelerated the demand for fossil fuels, metals, and non-metallic minerals . . . and will inevitably reduce the reserve life of finite resources. The competition for land between food and biofuels clearly played a part in rising food prices. And these demands in their turn are intimately linked to accelerating environmental impacts: rising carbon emissions, declining biodiversity, rampant deforestation, collapsing fish stocks, declining water supplies and degraded soils.[80]

The absurdity of projected growth models is also evident in assumptions about development. "If development means anything concretely [in traditional economics]," Daly writes, "it means a process by which the South becomes like the North in terms of consumption levels and patterns."[81] If 9 billion people had incomes similar to those of citizens in Europe today, then the average person's carbon intensity in 2050 would be about 55 times greater than today. If we allow for a 2 percent economic growth rate during this period, then the average carbon intensity would be 130 times higher.[82] This is utterly impossible in light of the consequences of climate change, but it reflects the prevailing logic of most economists and politicians who continue to embrace dead-end roads on which economics is divorced from ecology and the pursuit of relentless growth is seen as the key to prosperity.

If the earth spoke in plain English it would tell us something like this.

Help, I'm in trouble. Therefore, you're in trouble too. You are taking too many resources from me, using them up and spitting out waste I can't safely absorb. The collective weight of too many people, too much mining, drilling, and cutting, too much growth, too much consumption, too many chemicals applied to the land, too much water pollution, and too much waste is exhausting and poisoning me. It is also killing off species and warming the planet at alarming rates. The idea that you will grow your way

*out of this environmental mess is delusional. By the way, if I'm
not healthy you won't be either. And don't think technology will
save us. You've got value problems that technology alone can't
solve. We need a heavy-dose of humility and simplicity if humanity
is to flourish along with other creatures. We need a partnership
that binds together all species, respects limits, values equity, seeks
greater justice, preserves the commons, concerns itself with present and future generations, redefines prosperity, and focuses on
meaning and sustainability more than affluence and the quantity
of possessions.*

Or maybe the earth would simply quote Chief Seattle, "Whatever befalls
the earth, befalls the sons [and daughters] of the earth."

The earth is speaking loudly and clearly. Floods, droughts, global
warming, species loss, melting ice, land and water degradation, wildfires, heat waves, superweeds and superbugs, bizarre weather patterns
and other signs of environmental stress are among nature's tongues. The
ten warmest years on record have occurred since 1998. Tied for setting
the all-time mark were 2005 and 2010. "After enough repetitions of
shocking weather, we can't remain indefinitely shocked," Barbara Kingsolver writes. "When the Earth seems to raise its own voice to the pitch
of a gale, have we the ears to listen?"[83]

WHAT NOW?

The relentless pursuit of growth already has impoverished the environment and many hundreds of millions of people. It threatens to ignite
additional conflicts over shrinking resources, and it accelerates the pace
of climate change that could undermine life on earth as we know it.
"There are three levels of violence involved in non-sustainable development," Vandana Shiva writes. "The first is the violence against the
earth, which is expressed as the ecological crisis. The second is violence against people, which is expressed as poverty, destitution, and

displacement. The third is the violence of war and conflict, as the powerful reach for the resources that lie in other communities and countries for their limitless appetites."[84]

Set Clear Limits and Define Sustainability

Development is truly sustainable when it respects ecological limits, improves quality of life, and diminishes resource use. The good news is that there are alternative pathways that could end violence against the earth, reduce poverty, promote economic justice, restrain consumer appetites, reduce resource use, end resource wars, restore ecological health, and secure the social, spiritual, and economic well-being of present and future generations.

"Although there is an emerging political consensus on the desirability of something called sustainable development, this term—touted by many and even institutionalized in some places—is still dangerously vague," Daly writes. "Apparent agreement masks a fight over what exactly 'sustainable development' should mean—a fight in which the stakes are very high."[85] An economy pursuing sustainable development recognizes that the ecosystem is "finite, non-growing, and materially closed." It stabilizes total resource use, population size, and the amount of waste the ecosystem must absorb and keeps them "at ecologically sustainable levels."[86] It sets no limits on creativity, knowledge, culture, genetic inheritance, goodness, compassion, ethics, justice, or distribution of benefits. Within a steady-state economy each of these can help improve quality of life. It is also possible to improve technology, quality, product design, and product mix. It is the total aggregate stock of resources used that remains constant, not well-being. "If we use 'growth' to mean *quantitative change* and 'development' to refer to *qualitative change*, then we may say that a steady-state economy develops but does not grow, just as the planet earth, of which the human economy is a subsystem, develops but does not grow."[87]

Stabilize Population

One key to sustainability is reducing birth rates and stabilizing population. Hundreds of millions of women worldwide want but are denied access to family planning options because of poverty, politics, gender bias, and religious and cultural norms. Most population growth occurs in the developing world, where the populations are young and of childbearing age. Even if family size reflects replacement rates, there is a period of demographic delay in which the overall population grows for decades.

The basic parameters of solutions are clear. Expand access to family planning in the context of policies that meet essential needs because a measure of security reduces the need for larger families. Make family planning affordable, accessible, and applicable for both men and women. Educate and empower women and enhance their roles and skills within the economy and society. Redefine cultural norms and challenge religious teachings. Having many children is not the purpose of marriage, a sign of God's blessing, or proof of a man's virility. In some cases it is a rational choice given high levels of infant mortality. In many others it is a glaring sign of human arrogance and ecological stupidity.

The teachings and positions on family planning of the Catholic Church, some Muslim clerics, and other conservative religious groups are indefensible in today's world. It may have made sense to "be fruitful and multiply" in biblical times but not on an overcrowded, finite planet threatened by human excess. In developing countries the prospect of a demographic delay adds urgency to act in all the areas noted above. It also calls for delaying marriage and childbirth, spacing births properly, and limiting family size. One successful approach to changing cultural norms is to encourage family planning and delayed marriage through the actions of sympathetic soap opera characters. It is also imperative to stabilize population in developed countries where per capita consumption is higher and ecological footprints are heavier.

Another helpful step would be to stop holding family planning hostage to abortion politics. Anti-abortion advocates and their political allies frequently cut U.S. aid to international and domestic family planning programs, ostensibly because some groups include abortion counseling or services in their mix of family planning options. This politicization has devastating consequences, especially for poor women. It has resulted worldwide in hundreds of millions of additional unwanted pregnancies, higher rates of maternal mortality, increased poverty, and millions of unnecessary abortions. The Guttmacher Institute reports that in 2006 publicly financed family planning prevented nearly 2 million unwanted pregnancies and averted 810,000 abortions in the United States. Internationally it calculated that a 15 percent decline in support for the United Nations Population Fund (which doesn't fund abortions but does provide family planning) would result in nearly 2 million more unwanted pregnancies, 5,000 more maternal deaths, and 800,000 additional abortions.[88] The Guttmacher Institute also notes that unwanted pregnancies and abortions are declining in countries where abortion is legal and that 70,000 women die each year from illegal and oft-times botched abortions.[89] One thing is almost certain: In the not too distant future, population growth rates will decline. They will do so by death and disease if we stay on dead-end roads or because we have taken necessary steps to build sustainable societies.

Revitalize Local and Regional Food Systems

We have a tremendous opportunity to achieve sustainability as we abandon the dead-end road of industrial agriculture and embrace alternatives that encourage food security, food sovereignty, food justice, ecological diversity, and revitalization of local and regional food systems worldwide. Industrial agriculture claims it offers the only hope to feed a hungry world and keep pace with population growth. To better understand this view it is necessary to describe other reasons beyond the absence of effective family planning that help explain why global population has grown exponentially: Simple drugs, vaccines, and other health care advances mean that fewer children die and adults live longer; increases in food production allow a growing population to be fed, although due to poverty, maldistribution, and other factors nearly a billion people are hungry.

For more than sixty years diversified agricultural systems worldwide have given way to monocultures, and fossil fuel inputs have substituted for natural soil fertility. Although the industrial agricultural system increased yields of a few basic crops, it also sowed the seeds of future vulnerability because it caused and ignored negative ecological, social, and health impacts. There are three primary expressions of this vulnerability. First, the U.S. industrial food system has accumulated a stunning account of ecological debts: superweeds and superpests; water poisoned with residues from chemical pesticides, herbicides, and nitrogen fertilizers; run-off from centralized feed lots; soil erosion; dangerous use of antimicrobial drugs; oil dependency; depletion of aquifers; dead zones in the Gulf linked to corn and ethanol production.

A second vulnerability is the sobering prospect of disruptions in the fossil-fuel-intensive agricultural sector as the world deals with peak oil and moves from relative oil abundance to relative or absolute scarcity. Olivier De Schutter and Gaetan Vanloqueren note that the International Energy Agency "warned in 2009 that oil is running out far more quickly than previously predicted" and that "global production is likely to peak in about ten years." The implications for agriculture are clear:

> Modern agriculture is highly sensitive to oil prices. Our food relies on oil or gas at many stages: nitrogen fertilizers are made from natural gas, pesticides are made out of oil, agricultural machinery runs on oil, irrigation and modern food processing are highly energy-dependent, and food is transported over thousands of miles by road or air. While the exact impacts of peak oil on the availability and cost of both oil and natural gas are unknown, it will undoubtedly affect food security.[90]

Peak oil means steadily rising prices. It requires us and others throughout the world to change how food is produced and how far it travels to market. The emphasis will be on revitalizing local and regional agricultural systems, on fewer energy-intensive inputs, and on relocalizing diets. Community Supported Agriculture (CSAs), farmers markets, community-scale canning of local produce, family and neighborhood size root cellars, production of fruits and vegetables on public lands with public gleaning rights, organic agriculture, family-scale farms, and urban and roof-top gardens are some of the ways to enhance food security. Many communities are beginning to plan pathways to sustainability in a post-cheap-oil world in Transition Town or Transition Initiatives Movements.[91]

A third set of vulnerabilities is evident in distortions in agricultural systems worldwide that ironically stem from problems of overproduction. The drive to deal with U.S. agricultural surpluses resulted in short-sighted policies with serious ecological, economic, and public health consequences. Excess production of a few basic grains sparked a frantic search for what to do with surpluses. "Solutions" reinforced methods of unsustainable production and resulted in other damaging practices that had far-reaching consequences. Animals were fed lots of grain and people were encouraged to eat grain-fed meat. Beef cattle that have a marvelous capacity to turn grass into high quality meat were confined in centralized feed lots and fed grains. Ethanol plants absorbed about 40 percent of the U.S. corn crop. Highly processed corn also found its way into many thousands of food items, in many cases adding calories that contribute to obesity. And U.S. food aid was designed specifically to create foreign markets for U.S. agricultural commodities and to discourage local production in recipient nations. Practices that once served the purpose of absorbing price-deflating surpluses are now responsible for price spikes, food riots, obesity, and hunger. Many of these perverse practices are fueled by federal subsidies.

From the colonial period to today's trade agreements and structural adjustment programs, "developing" nations have been forced to ignore

diversified agriculture and rural development. As De Schutter and Vanloqueren write, the "orientation toward economic deregulation and priva-
tization" of the International Monetary Fund and World Bank "resulted
in a 25-year downsizing of public services and disinvestment in agricultural systems."[92] Many poor nations export commodities or specialty
crops at the expense of a healthy, diversified economy. Industrial agriculture's narrow focus on using chemically based inputs to produce a few
commodities in overabundance meant the neglect of other indigenous
crops and of small or subsistence producers. This flawed system has
clearly failed. Unfortunately, as hunger concerns and interest in developing country agriculture grow, the architects of dead-end roads generally
propose "solutions" based on the high-tech, industrial model.

Support Promising Alternatives

Fortunately, there are many positive examples of and articulate advocates
for alternative approaches that lead to sustainable agricultural systems.
"A growing number of experts are calling for a major shift in food security policies, and support the development of agro-ecology approaches,
which have shown very promising results where implemented," notes
Olivier De Schutter, the UN's special rapporteur on food.[93] "Agroecol-
ogy is the application of ecological science to the study, design, and
management of sustainable agriculture. It seeks to mimic natural ecological processes, and it emphasizes the importance of improving the entire
agricultural system, not just the plant."[94] According to writer and farmer
Jim Goodman, the IAAST report (see below) based on the research of
four hundred experts makes clear "that the best hope for ending hunger
lies with local, traditional, farmer controlled agricultural production, not
high tech industrial agriculture."[95]

The International Assessment of Agricultural Knowledge, Science
and Technology for Development (IAASTD) report on agriculture
has broad relevance for people committed to ecologically responsible
development.[96] It highlights the importance of food security and food

sovereignty. Food security is defined as "a situation that exists when all people, at all times, have physical, social, and economic access to sufficient, safe, and nutritious food that meets their dietary needs and food preferences for an active and healthy life." Food sovereignty is "the right of peoples and sovereign states to democratically determine their own agricultural and food policies." [97] These definitions have much in common with Robert Gottlieb and Anupama Joshi's definition of food justice "as ensuring that the benefits and risks of where, what, and how food is grown and produced, transported, and distributed, and accessed and eaten are shared fairly." [98]

Policies that encourage food security, food sovereignty, and food justice conflict sharply with standard economic theories and practices that promote economic growth, specialization, and expanded global trade as the key to development. "Generally, the adverse consequences of global changes have the most significant effects on the poorest and most vulnerable, who historically have had limited entitlements and opportunities for growth," the IAASTD report states. [99] The report is highly critical of high-tech, energy- and chemical-intensive approaches to increasing agricultural production, including biotechnology, because they ignore or exacerbate social, political, cultural, gender, legal, environmental, and economic problems that are the underlying causes of hunger, poverty, and ecological crises. "Historically the path of global agricultural development has been narrowly focused on increased productivity rather than on more holistic integration of natural resource management (NRM) with food and nutritional security," the report states. [100] "Higher level drivers of biotechnology R & D" may attract "investment in agriculture," it notes, but they "can also concentrate ownership of agricultural resources." [101] The report is also critical of the growing practice of diverting agricultural crops to fuel which displaces small land holders and "can raise food prices and reduce our ability to alleviate hunger throughout the world." [102]

Real solutions involve agro-ecological approaches that encourage increased food production and food security in a context of environmental sustainability and social justice. The agro-ecological approach recognizes that natural "resources, especially those of soil, water, plant, and animal diversity, vegetation cover, renewable energy sources, climate, and ecosystem services are fundamental for the structure and function of agricultural systems and for social and environmental sustainability, in support of life on earth."[103] Increasing food production, food security, food sovereignty, and social and ecological well-being are possible when we "recognize farming communities, farm households, and farmers as producers and managers of ecosystems."[104]

Key challenges are to meet "the need for food and livelihood security under increasingly constrained environmental conditions from within and outside the realm of agriculture and globalized economic systems." The goals served by "agricultural knowledge, science, and technology (AKST)" should be "to reduce hunger and poverty, to improve rural livelihoods, and to facilitate equitable environmentally, socially, and economically sustainable development."[105] High priority should be given to efforts to improve the capacity of "resource-poor farmers, women, and ethnic minorities"[106] and "to reduce poverty and provide improved livelihoods options for the rural poor, especially landless and peasant communities, urban, informal and migrant workers." This "will require a shift to nonhierarchical development models,"[107] a "revalorization of traditional and local knowledge,"[108] and a focus on nontraditional crops and largely ignored producers. "AKST investments can increase the sustainable productivity of major subsistence foods including orphan and underutilized crops, which are often grown or consumed by poor people."[109]

The report details other priority investments to enhance sustainability goals and reduce negative environmental impacts. These include: improved conservation and resource technologies; better techniques for organic and low-input agricultural systems; valuation of ecosystem services; reducing water pollution and increasing water use efficiency; biological controls of pests and pathogens and biological alternatives to agrochemicals; and significant reductions in fossil fuel use in the agricultural sector.[110] A key goal is to improve equity in the farm and rural sectors, especially more equitable access to land and water resources. Reward structures should also be in place so that ecosystem services are valued and farmers and rural residents benefit from ecologically responsible actions. The report calls for preferential investments in literacy, education and training that "contribute to reducing ethnic, gender, and other inequities" that would "advance development goals. Measurements of returns to investment require indices that give more information than GDP, and that are sensitive to environmental and equity gains."[111]

In sum, soft landings require us to revitalize and relocalize ecologically responsible agricultural systems worldwide. The good news is that there are far-reaching environmental, economic, and social benefits that flow from agricultural policies and practices that respect ecological limits. The United Nations report "Agro-ecology and the Right to Food," concluded that sustainable, small-scale farming could double food production in five to ten years in areas where most hungry people live.[112]

The basic contours of alternative policies and solutions are clear: revitalize local and regional agricultural systems; reject one-size-fits-all trade agreements that undermine food sovereignty and food security; encourage local production and consumption of food; enhance security of land tenure for small-scale farmers; invest in public goods, services, and infrastructure that support rural communities; eat foods in season; build up the natural fertility and health of soils; value equity; enhance the capacity of marginalized groups; focus on increasing production of indigenous crops; reject monocultures and emphasize diversity and resiliency; reduce use of fossil fuels and chemicals; protect water supplies and use water efficiently; reward conservation practices and recognize the monetary and ecological value of ecological services like wetlands and forests; reintegrate production of animals with crop production; avoid feed lots and concentration of waste; eat less meat and eat meat produced locally and sustainably; promote small, diversified farms; build a sustainable agricultural system in the context of comprehensive efforts to develop healthy rural communities; don't use food crops for energy production; reduce scale; preserve farmland and restrict urban encroachment; conserve; plan beyond peak oil; and simultaneously pursue goals of food security, ecological integrity, gender equality, and social justice.

End Poverty and Protect Ecological Systems

Sustainability also requires that we end poverty and restore and protect ecological systems. Lester Brown lays out a detailed "Eradicating Poverty Initiative," which meets the following basic social goals worldwide: universal primary education; adult literacy; school lunch programs and assistance to preschool children and pregnant women in the 44 poorest countries; reproductive health and family planning; and universal health care. He also details "Earth Restoration Goals" including reforesting the earth, protecting topsoil on cropland, restoring rangelands, stabilizing water tables, restoring fisheries, and protecting biological diversity. The price tag (about $187 billion a year) is modest relative to U.S. and global military spending levels.[113] Also, as UN Secretary-General Ban Ki-moon notes, "Maintaining and restoring our natural infrastructure can provide economic gains worth trillions of dollars each year. Allowing it to decline is like throwing money out the window."[114]

Address Climate Change and Build a Green Economy Now

Climate change is a consequence of human arrogance, disregard for ecological systems, and the failure to live within environmental constraints set by nature. It is potentially devastating to future generations because it involves tampering with the earth's vital ecosystems on which meaningful human life depends. Business interests have spent millions of dollars to create doubt about the science of global warming (as they did previously with tobacco) and to influence politicians who have been more than willing to thwart efforts to enact meaningful public policy alternatives.[115] Unfortunately, their successful efforts jeopardize the future.

Despite doubt in the public mind there is overwhelming scientific consensus that human activities that pour CO_2 and other greenhouse gases into the atmosphere are heating up the earth. Scientific points of uncertainty have to do with what level of CO_2 concentration in the atmosphere is safe, how quickly and deeply cuts need to be, and when we might cross tipping points that could trigger runaway warming with catastrophic consequences for future generations.

Scientists for many years presumed that CO_2 concentrations of 550 ppm in the atmosphere were relatively safe. The 2007 Intergovernmental Panel on Climate Control (IPCC) report reduced this to 450 ppm and worrisome trends since have convinced many scientists that 350 ppm is a safer bet. In the same report the IPCC called for CO_2 emission reductions of between 25 and 40 percent from 1990 levels by 2020. Actions taken by governments to date, especially by the United States, don't get close to that number. The United States, for example, offered to reduce U.S. carbon emissions by 4 percent from 1990 levels at the international conference in Copenhagen in December 2010.

Political leaders and some businesses fear that steps taken to address climate change will slow economic growth. Environmentalists and a few forward-thinking economists are aware that failure to act will have grave ecological and economic consequences and that the costs of inaction far outweigh the costs of proactive policies. Many climate scientists warn that without profound and immediate cuts in greenhouse gas emissions climate tipping points could be crossed that trigger irreversible warming. They see four grave threats: melting of the polar ice caps will accelerate a cycle of warming because water absorbs more heat than ice; thawing of snow and ice could release massive amounts of methane that have been locked in ice for many thousands of years (methane is a greenhouse gas many times more potent that CO_2); melting of the Greenland ice sheet could result in sea level rises that would create hundreds of millions of climate refugees; acidification of the ocean could undermine the food chain.

The 2007 IPCC report projects the earth's average temperature to rise during this century by 2–11.5 degrees Fahrenheit, with its best estimate being temperature rises of 3.2–7.1 degrees.[116] The report projects that sea levels will rise between 7 inches and 30.7 inches.[117] James Hansen projects that "business as usual" will result in a temperature rise between 3.6–7.2 degrees Fahrenheit making the world a "desolate place."[118] He warns that the last time "the Earth was five degrees warmer was three million years ago, when sea level was about eighty feet higher." This would result in hundreds of millions of climate refugees from New York to Bangladesh.[119]

There isn't much good news to report about climate change other than to say that the parameters of meaningful responses are relatively clear. Here it is probably more honest to say that soft landings *may* be possible. "Forget that this task of planet-saving is not possible in the time required," Paul Hawken says. "Don't be put off by people who know what is not possible. Do what needs to be done, and check to see if it was impossible only after you are done."[120] We can't know if doing all we can do will be enough. We do know what the consequences of inaction are likely to be, what we should be doing, and what constitutes a good-faith effort.

We need to green the economy and dramatically reduce the role of carbon-based fuels. Other vital steps to be taken include: conserve everything; consume less; retrofit existing buildings and build new ones efficiently; relocalize economies and produce essential goods locally and regionally with recycled materials and renewable energy resources; support reforestation efforts and adopt agricultural practices that capture carbon; emphasize efficiency, durability, and recyclability in all product designs; develop a green infrastructure including smart grids; maximize energy production based on wind, geothermal, solar, wave, and other renewable sources; quickly phase out coal plants and reject nuclear power; focus transportation on public transit; make modest use of cars (electric); promote trains not planes for transport and freight; reassess needs and wants; recycle and compost everything; decentralize energy and food systems; set firm caps on carbon emissions; raise the price of carbon through a carbon tax and distribute revenues to citizens on a per capita basis; require that cuts in carbon emissions take place within developed countries themselves rather than through offsets; model the transition to sustainability and then help poorer nations "leap-frog" to use of efficient, sustainable technologies; move to a steady-state economy; and set energy production goals within the framework of lifestyles that respect ecological needs and environmental constraints (not fantasy growth scenarios), and live within these boundaries.

Redefine Prosperity and Focus on Quality of Life to Reduce Ecological Footprints

Greening the economy is important but not enough. The "materialistic vision of prosperity must be dismantled," Jackson writes. We need "a different kind of vision for prosperity: one in which it is possible for human beings to flourish, to achieve greater social cohesion, to find higher levels of well-being and yet still to reduce their material impact on the environment."[121] This requires us to recognize that beyond "the provision of nutrition and shelter, prosperity consists in our ability to participate in the life of society, in our sense of shared meaning and purpose in our capacity to dream." The "developing" world will still need to focus on material growth to meet essential needs, but morally and ecologically it is imperative that we focus on quality of life measures. There are wonderful possibilities if we place flourishing at the heart of our conception of prosperity. As Jackson writes:

> Physical and mental health matter. Educational and democratic entitlements count too. Trust, security and a sense of community are vital to social well-being. Relationships, meaningful employment and the ability to participate in the life of society appear to be important almost everywhere. People suffer physically and mentally when these things are absent. Society itself is threatened

when they decline. The challenge for society is to create the conditions in which these basic entitlements are possible.[122]

We need to target public sector investments to promote low-carbon systems and infrastructures, protect ecological resources, and enhance energy security. As Jackson writes, we will need "high employment in low-carbon sectors."[123] Harvey Wasserman notes the potential for wind energy: "currently available wind turbines spinning between the Mississippi and the Rockies could generate 300 percent of the nation's electricity. There's sufficient potential in North Dakota, Kansas, and Texas alone to do 100 percent. Cost and installation times put nukes to shame."[124] The IPCC released a landmark report in May 2011, which says that renewable energy could account for nearly 80 percent of the world's energy within forty years if governments pursue appropriate policies at a modest projected yearly cost of about 1 percent of global production.[125]

Ultimately, soft landings depend on our willingness to accept ecological constraints, less materialism, and fewer jobs in production. Jobs will need to be shared and more jobs focused on non-material ways of improving community health and well-being. Providing libraries, parks, and green spaces, quality life-long education opportunities and quality health care, and enriching culture are some of the ways to enhance quality of life while reducing ecological footprints.

CONCLUSION

Climate change is more of a message than an issue. As Naomi Klein writes:

[It is] a symptom of a much larger crisis, one born of the central fiction on which our economic model is based: that nature is limitless, that we will always be able to find more of what we need, and if something runs out it can be seamlessly replaced by another resource that we can endlessly extract. But it is not just the atmosphere that we have exploited beyond its capacity to recover—we are doing the same to the oceans, to freshwater, to topsoil, and to biodiversity. The expansionist, extractive mindset, which has so long governed our relationship to nature, is what the climate crisis calls into question so fundamentally....Climate change is a message, one that is telling us that many of our culture's most cherished ideas are no longer viable.[126]

Economically and ecologically we have reached the end of the world as we know it and only alternative pathways can save us. Fortunately, unrealistic growth scenarios are not only impossible but unnecessary. There are pathways to soft landings and sustainability. As we will see in chapter 3, sustainability requires us to promote greater equity and revitalize politics to serve the common good.

Chapter 3

Equity, Politics,
and the Common Good

We must keep in mind that free institutions include not only the institution of individual freedom in the competitive marketplace (freedom from monopoly) but also the social, collective freedom to democratically enact rules for the common good. —HERMAN DALY[1]

All the developed countries I looked at provide health coverage for every resident, old or young, rich or poor. This is the underlying moral principle of the health care system in every rich country—every one, that is, except the United States.

—T. R. REID[2]

The evidence shows that reducing inequality is the best way of improving th0e quality of the social environment, and so the real quality of life, for all of us. . . . If you want to know why one country does better or worse than another, the first thing to look at is the extent of inequality.

—RICHARD WILKINSON AND KATE PICKETT[3]

INTRODUCTION

By most measures the United States is the most unequal of the world's developed countries, and it has the poorest safety net for those who fall through the cracks. In the previous chapter I described the need to reject unrealistic growth scenarios, respect ecological limits, build an ecologically responsible economy, and redefine prosperity. The present chapter examines the causes and consequences of inequality in the United States, the many benefits of promoting greater equity and the common good, and pathways to a more equitable society. Prosperity through perpetual growth is an illusion, and greening the economy is an essential but limited goal. Essential goods, services, wages, wealth, and jobs will need to be shared more equitably as part of a society committed to meeting the fundamental needs of present and future generations and serving the common good.

A bad news–good news pattern is evident here. When it comes to the economy and inequality, our nation is in deep trouble and dead-end roads that maintain disparities and court disaster are supported by powerful organized groups. Inequalities are so pronounced here, however, that alternative pathways offer authentic reasons for hope. It's the end of the world as we know it but soft landings are possible.

EVIDENCE OF INEQUALITY

Robert Reich identifies three stages of American capitalism. The first, roughly 1870–1929, was marked by increased concentration of wealth. The second from 1947 to 1975 was a period in which prosperity was more broadly shared. The third stage (1980–2010) once again saw increased concentrations of wealth.[4] "Over the last generation, more and more of the rewards of growth have gone to the rich and superrich," write political scientists Jacob S. Hacker and Paul Pierson in their book *Winner-Take-All Politics.* "The rest of America, from the poor through the upper middle class, has fallen further and further behind."[5]

Evidence is stark of a winner-take-all economy in which fabulous wealth and income gains have accrued a small segment of the U.S. population over the past thirty years. For example, the richest 1 percent of Americans in the late 1970s had less than 9 percent of the nation's total income. By 2010 they had nearly a quarter.[6] The elite 1 percent from 1979 until the eve of the 2007 economic crisis received 36 percent of all gains in household income. Between 2001 and 2006 they garnered more than 53 cents of every dollar of the nation's total income gains.[7] This actually understates the degree of economic concentration. Between 1979 and 2005 the richest tenth of 1 percent (about 300,000 Americans) received almost twice as great a share of the nation's income gains as the bottom 60 percent of the population combined (180 million people). Not surprisingly, income inequalities aggravate wealth inequalities. Between 1983 and 2004 only 10 percent of wealth gains went to the bottom 80 percent of Americans.[8] "These mind-boggling differences have no precedent in the forty years of shared prosperity that marked the U.S. economy before the late 1970s. Nor do they have any real parallel elsewhere in the advanced industrial world."[9]

We can see similar trends through a slightly different lens. Between 1979 and 2006 real household income in the United States rose almost 50 percent, but 90 percent of Americans benefited little or not at all. The average income of the poorest 20 percent rose about 10 percent over those twenty-six years from $14,900 to $16,500. The average gain of the middle 20 percent (those above the bottom 40 percent and below the top 40 percent) was about 21 percent as average income rose from $42,900 to $52,100. This may seem impressive but it amounts to a real gain of 0.7 percent a year during a time of robust economic growth and longer working hours for American workers. The top 1 percent during this same time saw their incomes rise by 260 percent![10] As Hacker and Pierson note, "The rich are getting fabulously richer while the rest of Americans are basically holding steady or worse." "Unequal growth has been very, very good for the have-it-alls."[11]

These trends preceded but helped to create the financial meltdown of 2007 and the ongoing economic crisis that followed. Reich describes coping mechanisms Americans used in a desperate attempt to hang on to a decent standard of living. Women entered the work force in large numbers, and their contribution to family income partially compensated for declining or stagnant wages among male workers. Americans also significantly increased the number of hours they worked. On average, typical Americans worked 350 hours more than their European counterparts, and U.S. households added 500 additional hours of paid work (twelve weeks) per year compared to 1979. And we lived off of savings or racked up debts. Many families used their houses as ATMs. "Between 2002 and 2007, American households extracted $2.3 trillion from their houses, putting themselves ever more deeply into the hole," Reich writes. "Eventually, of course, the debt bubble burst. With it, the last coping mechanism disappeared."[12] American families lost nearly 40 percent of their home equity between December 2006 and December 2008.[13]

As coping strategies faltered, anger exploded. But misdirected anger can substitute one dead-end road for another. Wealthy backers of the Tea Party, for example, attempted to channel public anger away from big business practices and business domination of politics. Occupy Wall Street, by way of contrast, honed in like a laser on the causes of inequality: concentrated wealth that led to concentrated political power.

TROUBLING INEQUALITIES

Widespread inequalities run counter to many religious and philosophical traditions. The sacred texts of Judaism, Christianity, and Islam condemn pervasive inequality, promote equity, and focus centrally on justice. The Hebrew prophets condemn the rich for exploiting the poor and promise that a society rooted in God's justice will be without poverty. Muslims are implored to strive for justice and share with the community. Jesus frames his ministry as good news to the poor and justice for the oppressed, warns of the dangers of wealth, urges followers to be peacemakers, welcomes outcasts, and implores us to share.

Siddhartha Gautama was raised in isolation and privilege. He encountered extreme poverty and sought enlightenment. This spiritual quest led him and his Buddhist followers to challenge the hereditary inequality of the Hindu caste system. Karl Marx was outraged by the opulence and excesses of the few who benefited from the industrial revolution that left huge majorities destitute and exploited. His critique of capitalism and defense of the working class are at least partially responsible for taming the worst aspects of capitalism. In his novel *The Jungle,* Upton Sinclair captured the hopelessness and misery of the American working class as the nineteenth century came to an end. His book educated and mobilized the public.

Thirty-some years later, John Steinbeck did much the same. Written in the shadows of the gilded age, *The Grapes of Wrath* seared the memory of the Great Depression into the body politic at a time when activist government in the form of the New Deal offered common people a sense of hope and possibility. Michael Harrington's explosive expose of poverty in the United States, *The Other America,* was published in 1962 and helped move forward an anti-poverty agenda that included Medicare, Medicaid, expanded social security, and food stamps. Troubling inequalities have been consistently condemned by popes and an impressive body of Catholic and Protestant social teachings. And liberation theologies that link faith to social justice have emerged in response to stark social and economic inequalities in Latin America and beyond.

I could offer other examples, but my basic point is that profound inequalities clash sharply with the sensibilities and ethical norms of many of the world's religious and philosophical traditions. They consistently prompt social critics and reform movements seeking greater equity and fairer distribution of economic and social benefits. We are living at the cusp of another historical moment in which levels of inequality are destructive and indefensible. Inequalities in the United States and worldwide are religiously and philosophically repugnant, economically problematic, and socially intolerable. They are particularly troubling in light of our challenges to meet the essential needs of all while using fewer resources and addressing climate change.

COMPETING VIEWS

Defenders of inequality say it is good for the economy and for society. This has been an article of faith for the Republican Party since at least 1980. It translates into public policies to lower taxes for corporations and wealthy Americans, restrict government's ability to regulate business, and cut social programs that help the poor. Defenders consider it wise to help U.S. companies and rich Americans because they invest, create jobs, and grow the economy. Inequality is also understood as the natural outgrowth of a merit-based society that rewards hard work, intelligence, and excellence and that encourages personal responsibility.

This defense of inequality is highly immoral when judged in light of the religious and philosophical views just noted. It also has little historical validation. It was a deregulated marketplace that led to the Great Depression and to the recent economic meltdown. Also, the idea that you can cut taxes on the wealthy and thereby stimulate the economy sufficiently to make up for lost tax revenues has been thoroughly discredited from the time of Reagan to the present. When the Congressional Budget Office ranked eleven strategies to stimulate the economy and create jobs, cutting taxes for the wealthy was at the bottom.[14] Policies wrapped in ideological garb serve the crass class interests of the privileged few. A group of wealthy Americans associated with Wealth for the Common Good notes that between 1960 and 2004 the top 0.1 percent of taxpayers saw their average share of income paid in federal taxes drop from 60 to 33.6 percent. If this small sliver of taxpayers who make more than $7 million a year were to pay federal taxes at the 1960 rate it would mean $281 billion a year in additional government revenues.[15] And, as we will see below, wealth translates into powerful political influence among Republicans and Democrats.

It is particularly outlandish to pursue policies to further concentrate wealth at a time when the gap separating the rich from the rest of us is unprecedented and in the midst of so many unmet needs. "At a time when the country faced profound challenges—healing America's ailing health-care system, improving the nation's schools to face the demands of a new century, coping with the looming financial strains associated with an aging population—Republicans insisted that the country's top priority was big tax reductions for those at the top," write Hacker and Paulson. "They did so even though the incomes of the rich, and their share of national income, had grown faster in the previous decade than at any time in at least a century."[16]

A second perspective on inequality is that we don't need to worry too much about inequality as long as we promote equality of opportunity. This modest liberal view calls for investments in quality education for all and training programs that improve worker skills. Unfortunately, these worthy goals do not begin to address the causes of inequality or to compensate for the political and economic advantages the rich enjoy.

A third view held by progressive economists is that widespread inequality and highly concentrated incomes and wealth aggravate many economic and social problems. Many people in an unequal society lack effective means to participate meaningfully in economic life. This stifles demand and leads to a spiral of falling consumption, rising unemployment, factory closings, reduced wages, and declining tax revenues. "When most of the gains from economic growth go to a small sliver of Americans at the top," Robert Reich writes, "the rest don't have enough purchasing power to buy what the economy is capable of producing."[17] "We have become so unequal as a nation," Barbara Ehrenreich writes, "that we increasingly occupy two different economies—one for the rich and one for everyone else—and the latter economy has been in a recession, if not a depression, for a long, long time."[18] Adding insult to injury the rich can insulate themselves from the social decline their greed and privileges induce. As Reich notes:

> Across the nation, the most affluent Americans have been seceding from the rest of the nation into their own separate geographical communities with tax bases (or fees) that can underwrite much

higher levels of services. They have moved into office parks and gated communities, and relied increasingly on private security guards instead of public police, private spas and clubs rather than public parks and pools, and private schools (or elite public ones in their own upscale communities) for their children rather than the public schools most other children attend. Being rich means having enough money that you don't have to encounter anyone who isn't. The middle-class and the poor, meanwhile, rely on public services whose funding is ever more precarious: schools whose classrooms are more crowded; public parks and libraries open fewer hours and often less attended to; and buses and subways that are more congested. The adjective "public" in public services has come to mean "inadequate."[19]

Another downside to inequality is that the rich don't spend much of their inflated earnings. This places a further drag on the economy and adds incentive for the rich to engage in risky speculation of the kind that resulted in the 2007 economic collapse. Les Leopold writes:

For starters, "we" didn't create this mess. Wall Street did, with the help of politicians who pushed through financial deregulation and an increasingly regressive tax structure that put outrageous sums of money in the hands of a few. Freed from regulators and flooded with money, Wall Street bankers went crazy. And before long, our economy crashed. . . . With so much wealth in hand, the super-rich literally ran out of tangible goods and service industries to invest in. There simply was too much capital seeking too few real investments. And what a honey pot that proved to be for Wall Street's financial engineers! Freed from any limits on constructing complex new financial products, hedge funds and too-big-to-fail banks and investment houses created an alphabet soup of new securities with the sky-high yields the super-rich craved.[20]

Perhaps the most damaging consequence of inequality is that when wealth and incomes are concentrated so too is political power. Powerful corporations and wealthy Americans subvert popular democracy and use the political arena to reinforce their privileges, institutionalize their gains, and block necessary reforms. They were aided by a Supreme Court decision in 2010 that ruled that the government cannot ban or limit political spending by corporations in candidate elections.[21]

A fourth view on inequality is that it has many negative economic and social consequences and that greater equity offers profound benefits to individuals and to society. As Richard Wilkinson and Kate Pickett demonstrate convincingly in their book *The Spirit Level: Why Greater Equality Makes Societies Stronger*, the defining characteristic that determines health and social well-being and that limits social progress in all countries is "the amount of inequality."[22] In the United States particularly and developed countries generally, there are few additional benefits to economic growth but far-reaching benefits to greater equality. Greater equity is especially vital in the search for improved quality of life and an ecologically responsible prosperity that takes seriously climate change and other environmental constraints.

There are important differences among these diverse perspectives on inequality. Not surprisingly, defenders hold significantly dissonant views from the others. I am most interested, however, in conflicts between progressive economists like Robert Reich and people like Tim Jackson, Richard Wilkinson, and Kate Pickett who have deeper ecological sensibilities. Reich sees rightly that inequality is bad economics, and there will be no enduring economic recovery or sustained economic growth without fairer distribution of the economy's benefits. The others agree that inequality makes for bad economics and they recognize the need for a more just economy. However, they also understand the need for deeper economic changes in the context of ecological limits and the need to address climate change. They want to move beyond economic growth to a different kind of economy that promotes an alternative form of prosperity. It is within their framework that soft landings become possible.

THE POLITICS OF INEQUALITY

The degree of inequality in the United States today is unusual. Over the past thirty years we have moved to the top of advanced industrial countries in terms of inequality and the share and pace at which the richest 1 percent has claimed income gains. The only other time in our nation's history that inequality was this pronounced was during the gilded age immediately prior to the Great Depression. "If there were a gold medal for inequality, the United States would win hands down," labor economist Richard B. Freedom writes. "Standard measures show that the United States more closely resembles a developing country than an advanced country on this measure of economic performance."[23]

The obvious question is why, and the answer is surprisingly simple: politics. As Hacker and Pierson note, "our current crisis is merely the latest in a long struggle rooted in the interplay of American democracy and American capitalism."[24] In this latest go-around, well-organized corporations and wealthy Americans have effectively used government to rewrite "the rules of American politics and the American economy in ways that have benefited the few at the expense of the many."[25] They have enacted policies or blocked necessary reforms with highly effective results, systematically and intentionally redistributing wealth and income upward while undermining the political influence and economic well-being of average Americans.

Hacker and Pierson's fundamental claim is that government "has had a huge hand in nurturing America's winner-take-all economy." You can't explain America's radical shift of income and wealth to the privileged few over the past thirty years as consequences of globalization, changing technology, or differences in education or skill levels. These are sideshows in a much bigger drama. "To uncover the path to winner-take-all requires seeing the transformation of American government over the past generation, a transformation that has *fundamentally changed what government does, and whom it does it for*."[26]

Over the past thirty years the federal government has used two primary mechanisms to fuel the winner-take-all economy. It has acted deliberately to insure economic gains for America's superrich, and it has deliberately failed to act as a way of blocking needed reforms. It is true that "a large number of new laws that greatly exacerbate inequality *have* been created." It is also true "that big legislative initiatives are not the only way to reshape how an economy works and whom it works for. Equally, if not more, important is what we will call 'drift'—systematic, prolonged failures of government to respond to the shifting realities of a dynamic economy." The story of "America's winner-take-all economy isn't just about political leaders actively passing laws to abet the rich, but also about political leaders studiously turning the other way (with a lot of encouragement from the rich) when fast moving economic changes make existing rules and regulations designed to rein in excess at the top obsolete."[27]

Among the sins of commission are deregulation of financial markets and changes in the tax code. Deregulating finance created enormous profit opportunities from derivatives and other speculative instruments that Warren Buffett called "weapons of mass destruction."[28] As Hacker and Pierson note, "government policy not only failed to push back against the rising tide at the top of finance, corporate pay, and other winner-take-all domains, but also repeatedly promoted it. Government put its thumb on the scale hard."[29] Elected officials also aided the rich by actively carrying out "a three-decades-long tax-cutting spree."[30] Congress took specific measures to: reduce progressivity; cut tax rates for wealthy individuals and corporations; provide loopholes that "use intricate partnerships, off-shore tax havens, and other devices that skirt or cross legal lines;" allow earnings from speculative investments to be taxed at lower rates; gut the estate tax; and cripple oversight so that roughly one out of every six tax dollars owed goes unpaid. The cumulative result of these actions is that "the very, very, very rich—have enjoyed by far the greatest drop in their tax rates."[31] "It is as if the government had developed the economic policy equivalent of smart bombs, except these bombs carry payloads of cash for their carefully selected recipients."[32]

Examples of sins of omission (drift) include: lax enforcement of labor laws; failure to enact measures such as the Free Choice Act, which would make it easier for willing workers to join unions without risk or harass-ment; blocking efforts to regulate corporate governance or set limits or guidelines for executive (CEO) pay; failure to re-regulate Wall Street after it became clear that risky speculative investment schemes put the economy at risk and allowed firms to gamble with other peoples' money without accountability; maintaining an inadequate minimum wage; and blocking efforts to roll back tax breaks, address climate change, and enact meaningful health care reforms. Another example of drift is that corporate influence within Congress has been sufficient to block efforts to close loopholes that allow many of America's largest and most prof-itable corporations to pay little or no taxes on their enormous profits. America's top hundred companies paying taxes at the 35 percent rate designated by U.S. tax law would result in additional yearly federal rev-enues of $150 billion, enough to wipe out the collective budget deficits of all fifty states.[33]

Politics, according to Hacker and Pierson, is "organized combat," and over the past thirty years powerful business groups and wealthy Ameri-cans have won battle after battle. They organize effectively and domi-nate Washington decision making. They are extremely well funded and well positioned to enact policies that serve their interests and to block reforms that challenge them. When it comes to seeking influence, they dramatically outspend all rivals, including advocacy groups and labor. They invest not only in elections but in think tanks that promote their ideas (they built "idea factories, rapidly and on a massive scale").[34] They also focus on grassroots mobilizations, and most importantly, effective lobbying. "Of the billions of dollars now spent every year on politics, only a fairly small fraction is directly connected to electoral contests. The bulk of it goes to lobbying—sustained, intense efforts to shape what happens in Washington."[35] Corporations and the wealthy care about who is elected, but their principal concern is to influence enough of the people who have been elected to effectively represent their interests. "The foremost obstacle to sustainable reform is the enormous imbalance in organizational resources between the chief economic beneficiaries of the status quo and those who seek to strengthen middle-class democracy."[36]

Other structural and procedural limitations within the Washington decision-making process make it difficult to overcome the advantages of the well-organized rich and powerful. The U.S. Senate is a very unrepresentative body. It has an "astonishing bias in favor of small states." And "racial and ethnic minorities, concentrated disproportionately in a few big states, are wildly underrepresented in the Senate."[37] The practical result is that the Senate has a built-in conservative bias that effectively disenfranchises huge numbers of people who care deeply about greater equality, the well-being of workers, and social justice.

The rules of the Senate, at least as they have functioned in recent years, allow use of filibusters, which means that sixty votes are needed to move legislation forward. This makes the filibuster an effective instrument to block progressive legislation and prevent needed reforms (drift). "Grafted onto the worsening malapportionment of the Senate, the de facto requirement that all legislation obtain sixty votes means that senators representing even small slices of the population or distinctly minority opinions can tie the institution into knots."[38] When you add the dimension of extreme polarization of U.S. politics with "the prolific use of the filibuster [you have] a perfect recipe for winner-take-all politics."[39] Now that the winner-take-all economy is in place the main strategy to defend it is often a politics of No.

Another structural factor that assists the rich and powerful is the revolving door that sends former members of Congress or their key staff

into well funded lobbying firms and sends influence and access back
to Washington. Also, the failure to enact meaningful campaign finance
reforms and the Supreme Court's determination that money is free speech
provide untold advantages to the wealthy to influence public policies in
favor of their own privileges.

Perhaps most important, Hacker and Pierson convincingly document
that pleasing wealthy donors and organized big business interests is now
the main preoccupation of *both* political parties. "The story of Republicans and Democrats is not black and white, but black and gray. In promoting the winner-take-all economy, Republicans proved zealots."[40]
Republicans over the past thirty years purged moderates from their ranks
and functioned in lock step on most issues. Their coalition was extremely
well funded and it wedded the interests of corporate America—tax cuts,
deregulation, social cut-backs, with those of cultural conservatives. "In
the new GOP's economic cookbook, all the pages bore the same recipe,
whether there was war or peace, recession or booming growth, high
deficits or low." The answer "always came back the same: tax cuts for
the rich."[41]

Democrats, on the other hand, were "in the awkward position of need-
ing to reconcile conflicting party identities. Were they the party of the
little guy and organized labor or a reliable partner in business?"[42] They
were "cross-pressured on economic issues."[43] A quote from Hacker and
Pierson reveals the untenable nature of this schizophrenic position, the
political equivalent to the religious admonition that you cannot serve
God and mammon:

> Wealthier Americans are less supportive of economic redistribu-
> tion and measures to provide economic security. They are less sup-
> portive of Medicare and Social Security. They are more supportive
> of tax cuts, especially cuts in taxes on dividends and capital gains.
> They are markedly less supportive of health insurance expan-
> sions financed by an increase in taxes—in fact income is a better
> predictor on this vital issue than party affiliation. Unlike poorer

Americans, however, wealthier Americans can back their positions up with serious money.[44]

Democrats live under a broader tent and lack the will and unity to counter the winner-take-all economy even when they are in the majority. Some receive solid support from labor, but this means less and less as labor's clout declines within the party and the contours of the winner-take-all economy. Many southern Democrats are functionally moderate Republicans at best. They rarely support meaningful reforms and are well-positioned to block them. Some Democrats are progressive on some or even many issues but are elected in states with particular business interests that they champion out of conviction or the will to survive. Competing interests mean that "the Democrats had a strong, organized faction pulling toward the positions of the other party."[45] "Even grudging or quiet support from a handful of Democrats—particularly well-placed ones—could make a huge difference. Such allies could help keep issues off the agenda, substitute symbolic initiatives for real ones, add critical loopholes, or insist on otherwise unnecessary compromises with the GOP."[46] Time after time enough Democrats join forces with Republicans to carry out business friendly policies or to block needed reforms. Hacker and Pierson explain how and why this happens:

> On critical economic issues, business interests could often count on a handful of moderate Democrats to complement the expected solid block of Republicans. In many cases, this was more than enough. Yet there was another group that expanded the conservative coalition . . . : Republicans for a Day. "Republicans for a Day" were Democrats, even "fighting liberal" Democrats like Chuck Schumer, who defected from the party on specific economic issues in deference to powerful local interests. . . . Each state economy has its 800-pound gorillas who command respect. That state's Democrats, if they hope to survive, will provide it.[47]

Beyond the dilemmas and financial challenges facing individual Democrats was a deeper structural crisis: As business dramatically increased its organizational clout, the Democratic Party found itself with serious financial deficiencies relative to its well-funded, ardently pro-business Republican rival. The fact that "permanent, relentless fundraising became a fixture of American politics"[48] not only pushed individual Democrats to cater to wealthy donors and business interests in their states, it also pushed the party as a whole to pursue business friendly policies. "Forced to deal with a much more organized and assertive business community and facing powerful financial incentives to seek accommodation, the Democratic Party apparatus reached out to corporate donors as never before."[49] As a result "Democrats at the commanding heights of their party were increasingly eager to show their friendliness to business and, especially, Wall Street."[50] In financial terms this proved a highly effective strategy. Money poured into Democratic coffers from many business sources, including the finance and pharmaceutical sectors. The dramatic tilt in favor of wealthy Americans and towards powerful business interests influenced profoundly the Democratic Party and American politics.

As the "organizational heft of business continued to grow," Democrats faced "greater incentives than ever to be responsive to the new economy's big winners."[51] "In all the critical policy ventures enabling the winner-take-all economy, Democrats played a supportive part."[52] For example, many Democrats provided critical support for the GOP's aggressive tax cutting. "This was not just a matter of providing bipartisan cover. In crucial cases, Democratic support made the initiatives possible."[53] In other areas, such as financial deregulation and serving Wall Street, Democrats took the lead.[54] "With labor atrophied, mass-membership federations crumbling, and voters disorganized, the incentives for resisting the deregulatory wave were meager compared with the financial rewards."[55] Overall, Democrats played key roles or joined Republicans to protect CEO pay; gut the estate tax; enact or extend tax cuts for the wealthy; block climate change legislation; limit the scale and effectiveness of health care reform; distort the economic stimulus package in favor of business rather than recovery; undermine labor initiatives; cut social programs; and we might add, although not addressed by Hacker and Pierson, squander the nation's resources on militarism and war.

Because Democrats have morphed into another business-dominated party, they have little to offer the majority of Americans, who are being hurt by the perfect storm of winner-take-all politics serving the winner-take-all economy. "During the heyday of the winner-take-all economy, the Democrats' capacity to improve the financial balance sheet of the middle class steadily deteriorated. The party's own balance sheets, however, just kept looking better and better. The continued effort to reorient party practices to winner-take-all realities was accompanied by a slow march toward financial parity with the GOP's national organizations."[56] Financial gains came with significant collateral damages. "Democrats lost ground among white working-class voters not in spite of economic issues but because of them."[57] Hacker and Pierson quote political analyst George Packer:

> Social issues like abortion, guns, religion, and even (outside the South) race had little to do with the shift. Instead . . . it was based on a judgment that—during years in which industrial jobs went overseas, unions practically vanished, and working-class incomes stagnated—the Democratic Party was no longer much help.[58]

Rising political cynicism is a consequence of Democrats conforming to the rules of winner-take-all politics in service to the winner-take-all economy. "Democrats faced less and less demand to present a sharp, populist economic message, and more and more pressure to refrain from such a position. They responded with a crouched economic posture that offered little of appeal to the middle class." I got a lot of puzzled looks when I told friends shortly after the election of Barack Obama that I feared he would do more damage to progressive politics than any other president. I reasoned that the Democrats' huge electoral gains resulted from two major factors. Many Americans disliked intensely what our nation had become. We longed to come out of the period I call the "Great Revulsion." We were tired of war, tired of torture, tired of climate change denial, and we worried about the economy and the future. Many also resonated with Obama's message of hope and change. People longed for reasons to hope, many wanted deep changes, and some worked tirelessly to get Obama elected because they thought *he* would be the instrument of change.

I thought this would end badly, at least in the short term. For many reasons outlined by Hacker and Pierson. I knew the policies of Obama and the Democrats were likely to be mediocre at best. They would clash sharply with the campaign rhetoric of hope and change and with what effective solutions and the historical moment actually demanded. The inevitable results of this wide gap between rhetoric, expectation, need, and reality would be to discredit progressive politics (associated now with Obama's weak and failed policies) and to foster political cynicism. This is something the Republicans understood well when they adopted a unified strategy of undermining all reform efforts. I believe it was comedian Bill Maher who said that after the election Democrats moved to the right and Republicans into a mental institution. In this case, however, the inmates had a clear strategy to benefit from the political cynicism they fostered along with their Democratic accomplices.

The final core argument of Hacker and Pierson is that winner-take-all politics is a human construct that can and must be altered. The problem is politics and "because it is domestic politics, not global economic trends, that matter most, the future is within our control. This is the very good news that this book delivers."[59]

POSSIBILITIES:
THE IMPORTANCE OF EQUITY

The rather depressing evidence of inequality and its causes presents us with another bad news–good news scenario. The bad news is that the

United States is one of the most unequal of all countries and among developed nations it ranks dead last in many measures of social well-being. The good news is that the magnitude of present inequalities amplifies prospects for meaningful alternatives. Inequality is so pronounced, winner-take-all politics so dysfunctional, and greater equity so beneficial that we have ample imaginative and political space to promote a meaning-based, ecologically sustainable, and equitable society. Our central task in the coming years is to improve quality of life and build sustainable societies that broadly share the benefits of an ecologically responsible economy.

Greater equity will make it possible to shrink the economy and resource use while improving quality of life. Worldwide billions of people have benefited little from economic growth because of inequality. Within the United States nearly all income and wealth gains over the past thirty years have gone to a privileged few. There is also abundant evidence that we are hitting an ecological wall that discredits the idea that future prosperity will be the fruit of economic growth. Equity is important because our core economic and ecological challenge is to do much better with less. In developed countries like the United States, future prosperity will be measured by our capacity to meet essential material needs in an ecologically responsible way and improve quality of life in non-material ways by cultivating and enhancing culture, creativity, compassion, service, and meaning. This will require stronger ties between ecology and social justice with a focus on addressing core needs, distributing benefits equitably, and using fewer resources.

There is abundant evidence that a healthy society requires a solid material foundation, but once essential needs are met there is little or no benefit to continued economic growth. As David Korten notes, once "a basic level of material well-being is achieved, the major improvements in our health and happiness come not from more money and consumption, but rather from relationships, cultural expression, and spiritual growth."[60] Richard Wilkinson and Kate Pickett write that in terms of life expectancy and happiness "the important gains are made in the earlier stages of economic growth, but the richer a country gets, the less getting still richer adds to the population's happiness." They note that in developed countries there is no benefit to doubling real incomes, whereas in poorer countries such economic gains matter greatly.[61]

There are many benefits to living in a more equitable society and many negative consequences of living in a highly unequal one. Wilkinson and Pickett found that health problems and social dysfunction are more common in countries with bigger income inequalities. These two were "extraordinarily closely related" and had much more to do with "inequality rather than to average living standards."[62] Overall they found that inequality was associated with lower levels of empathy and trust; less cooperation and community cohesiveness; higher incidences of mental illness and drug and alcohol addiction; gender inequalities in terms of political participation, employment and earnings, and social and economic autonomy; greater anxiety, fear, and stress; more status competition; lower life expectancy; higher infant mortality; higher incidences of obesity; lower self-esteem; increases in social distances and social stratification and greater concentrations of poverty; poor educational performance and lower literacy rates; psychologically damaging shame and stigma among the poor; more teenage births; more violence and homicides; poorer health outcomes; higher imprisonment rates and more punitive prison practices; less generosity, including fewer funds for foreign aid; and lower social mobility.[63] "More unequal countries also seem to be more belligerent internationally."[64]

For nations, more equality means better social health and inequality means more social problems. In all countries the defining characteristic that determines health and social problems is "the amount of inequality"[65] and the "evidence shows that reducing inequality is the best way of improving the quality of the social environment, and so the real quality of life for all of us."[66] Problems are three to ten times worse in unequal societies and these problems hurt whole populations, not just the poor.

The "prevailing assumption" is that "greater equality helps those at the bottom. . . . The truth is that the vast majority of the population is harmed by greater inequality."[67] Equal societies do better in almost all areas compared to unequal ones. "If for instance, a country does badly on health, you can predict with some confidence that it will also imprison a larger proportion of its population, have more teenage pregnancies, lower literacy scores, more obesity, worse mental health, and so on. Inequality seems to make countries socially dysfunctional across a wide range of outcomes."[68] Not surprisingly given its status as gold medal winner in inequality, the United States does poorly on many social indicators compared to other more equal nations. It is also true that within the United States there is a high correlation between worse social problems and levels of inequality. More equal states fair much better than unequal states. Greater equity would allow us to solve many pressing problems and enhance the prospects for soft landings. Wilkinson and Pickett write:

> The best way of responding to the harm done by high levels of inequality would be to reduce inequality itself. . . . Reducing inequality would increase the wellbeing and quality of life for all of us. Far from being inevitable or unstoppable, the sense of deterioration in social wellbeing and the quality of social relations in society *is* reversible. Understanding the effects of inequality means that we suddenly have a policy handle on the wellbeing of whole societies.[69]

Promoting equity is of greater importance given the vital need to take seriously environmental constraints and global warming. As Wilkinson and Pickett write: "We are the first generation to have to find new answers to the question of how we can make further improvements in the real quality of human life. What should we turn to if not to economic growth?"[70] Equity increases the likelihood that we can meet quality of life goals while dramatically reducing carbon emissions and resource use.

> If, to cut carbon emissions, we need to limit economic growth severely in the rich countries, then it is important to know that this does not mean sacrificing improvements in the real quality of

life—in the quality of life as measured by health, happiness, friend-ship and community life, which really matters. However, rather than simply having fewer of all the luxuries which substitute for and pre-vent us recognizing our more fundamental needs, inequality has to be reduced simultaneously. We need to create more equal societies able to meet our real social needs. Instead of policies to deal with global warming being experienced simply as imposing limits on the possibilities of material satisfaction, they need to be coupled with egalitarian policies which steer us to new and more fundamental ways of improving the quality of our lives. The change is about a historic shift in the sources of human satisfaction from economic growth to a more sociable society.[71]

POLICY IMPLICATIONS

There are practical policies involving budgets, taxes, health care, and social security that will help us build an equitable society that is ecologi-cally and fiscally sustainable, meets essential needs, enhances quality of life, and maximizes non-material aspects of prosperity. Contrary to pub-lic perceptions, it would be relatively easy to move from budget deficits to abundance so that the focus of government can shift from managing austerity to building a better society and sustainable world. The nation's present and future budget troubles are caused by four imminently solv-able problems: runaway military spending; an unfair tax system; rising costs of the social security system (this as actually a problem several decades out); and rising health care costs. Addressing these would solve budget problems, greatly improve prospects for soft landings, meet essential needs, and help establish a firm foundation for a materially suf-ficient, meaning-based society:

It is possible to dramatically reduce U.S. military spending while enhancing security (see chapter 5). Chris Hellman of the National

Priorities Project estimated in 2011 that since September 11, 2001, the United States had spent nearly $8 trillion for national security.[72] Much of this spending was unnecessary or counterproductive, which means with better priorities we could free up many hundreds of billions of dollars each year for other purposes.

Reestablishing a progressive, fair tax system will also significantly increase government revenues. The group Wealth for the Common Good lays out a series of responsible tax policy changes that would generate "over $450 billion in federal annual revenue from those with the greatest capacity to pay."[73] A modest tax on stock trades and financial transactions would discourage destructive speculation while increasing government revenues by $150 billion a year.[74] Taking the simple step of eliminating the cap on the social security payroll tax will insure the system's solvency. At present, workers pay into social security only on incomes up to $106,800. Subjecting all income from all sources to the social security tax and capping benefits will give all workers retirement security for generations to come.

Another vital step towards financial solvency and social well-being is to remove profit from the health care sector, something all other developed countries already do. This would both save money and make universal health coverage affordable for all. Journalist T. R. Reid traveled the world examining why and how other countries deliver affordable health care and the United States doesn't. He found that although the United States spends about twice as much per capita on health care "almost all advanced countries have better national health statistics than the United States does." Not only that, "we force 700,000 Americans into bankruptcies each year because of medical bills. In France, the number of medical bankruptcies is zero. Britain: zero. Japan: zero. Germany: zero."[75] Reid notes that more than "twenty thousand Americans die in the prime of life each year from medical problems that could be treated because they can't afford to see a doctor." These deaths and bankruptcies don't happen in any other developed country because such outcomes are immoral and therefore intolerable.[76]

Reid found that there were three distinctive approaches to health systems used by other nations to provide efficient, affordable care. Great Britain, New Zealand, and Cuba practice socialized medicine. Health care is provided through government-owned hospitals and government-employed health care workers paid from tax revenues. Canada and Taiwan have "single payer" systems. Citizens rely on private-sector providers but the government pays all the bills financed with tax revenues. This reduces red-tape bureaucracy and significantly reduces the costs of administering health care compared to the myriad costs associated with private insurance providers in the United States. Germany, the Netherlands, Japan, and Switzerland provide universal coverage using private doctors, private hospitals, and private insurers.

The United States, as Reid notes, has some aspects of these other systems: the Veteran's Administration is an example of socialized medicine and Medicare is a single payer system. These programs have the best health care outcomes, lowest costs, and greatest patient satisfaction.[77] Unfortunately, there is a key difference between private insurance in the United States and elsewhere: "foreign health insurance plans exist only to pay people's medical bills, not to make a profit. The United States is the only developed country that lets insurance companies profit from basic health coverage."[78]

We are also the only nation that allows health insurance and pharmaceutical-related industries to use some of their astronomical profits to buy congressional influence and undermine meaningful reforms. Hacker and Pierson describe how Republicans and Democrats prevented serious reforms during the Obama administration. "Tellingly, the administration focused much of its energy from the outset on cutting deals with powerful industry groups—drug companies, hospitals, and the insurance industry in particular."[79]

The group Physicians for a National Health Program (PNHP) describes problems with "reforms" that provide greater profit opportunities for private insurers. "Instead of eliminating the root of the problem—the profit-driven, private health insurance industry—this costly new legislation will enrich and further entrench these firms. The bill would require millions of Americans to buy private insurer's defective products and turn over to them vast amounts of public money." PNHP notes that polls indicate that nearly two-thirds of Americans express support for a single-payer system as do 59 percent of U.S. physicians.[80] There is a "genuine remedy in plain sight. Sooner rather than later, our nation will adopt a single-payer national health insurance program, an improved Medicare for all. This will assure truly universal, comprehensive and affordable care to all." A *St. Louis Post Dispatch* editorial agrees. It acknowledged that "everyone who has studied the deficit problem has agreed that it's actually a health care problem—more specifically, the cost of providing Medicare benefits to an aging and longer-living population." The best solution is not to deny people health care or shift costs onto consumers but rather take steps to reduce "spiraling health care costs." "This is what a single-payer health care system would do, largely by taking the for-profit players (insurance companies for the most part) out of the loop." "Eventually," the editorial concludes, "the United States will have a single-payer plan. But we'll waste a lot of money and time getting there."[81]

The collective impact of implementing these policies would be significant. Adequate resources would be available: to support the transition to a sustainable economy; to invest in nonmaterial quality-of-life improvements in areas such as education, art, music, public parks, libraries, and community centers; and to provide a solid foundation for social well-being through provision of quality health care and social security for all citizens.

REVITALIZING POLITICS

It is necessary to revitalize politics and reign in moneyed interests because dysfunctional politics is a leading cause of inequality. The failure of winner-take-all politics in service to a winner-take-all economy could inspire a shared vision of a more equitable, sustainable, and meaning-based society and give rise to a broad-based social movement capable of demanding meaningful reforms. As David Korten writes, we have "an opportunity to mobilize political support for a new economy that shifts our economic priorities from making money for rich people to creating better lives for all and that reallocates our economic resources from destructive, or merely wasteful, uses to beneficial ones."[82]

Writing in the context of Washington's failure to enact meaningful climate change legislation, Naomi Klein highlights the key lesson learned by groups such as 350.org, a lesson that has relevance for each of the issues discussed above: "trying to win this battle by lobbying elites behind closed doors is a disastrously losing strategy." The "real task," she writes, "is to build the kind of mass movement that politicians cannot afford to ignore. That means showing how making the deep emission cuts that science demands is not some dour punishment that will destroy our economy (as the Koch-funded right is perpetually claiming) but rather our best chance of fixing an economic system that is failing us on every level."[83]

In *The Spirit Level,* Wilkinson and Pickett write that when surveyed, a large majority of Americans "wanted society to 'move away from greed and excess toward a way of life more centered on values, community and family,'" but they felt isolated.[84] Surveys also show that Americans significantly underestimate the degree of inequality in the United States and overwhelmingly say they would prefer to live in a more egalitarian society. For example, when respondents were given a choice to live in one of two unnamed countries, one in which the richest 20 percent controlled 84 percent of the wealth (in actuality the United States) or one in which they controlled 36 percent of the wealth (in actuality Sweden), 92 percent chose Sweden's wealth distribution. According to the study's authors: "All demographic groups—even those not usually associated with wealth redistribution such as Republicans and the wealthy—desired a more equal distribution of wealth than the status quo."[85]

Soft landings *are* possible, but we need a shared vision that inspires action. "Mainstream politics . . . has abandoned the attempt to provide a shared vision capable of inspiring us to create a better society. As voters we have lost sight of any collective belief that society could be different. Instead of a better society, the only thing almost all of us strive for is to better our own position as individuals—within the existing society." But it doesn't have to be this way. A better understanding of possibilities "could transform politics and quality of life for all of us. It would change our experience of the world around us, change what we vote for, and change what we demand from our politicians."[86]

Jeffrey Sachs writes that corporations "have become a threat to society by using their lobbying power to dictate the terms of legislation and regulation. The license to operate as a company does not include a license to pollute our politics."[87] What greater unifying challenge could we imagine than saving the planet for future generations, addressing climate change, restoring the ecological health of the earth, building sustainable economies, and modeling meaning-based prosperity? Wilkinson and Pickett's analysis is profoundly hopeful. They write that with greater equality "it is possible to improve the quality of life for everyone in modern societies." There "is a way out of the woods for all of us."[88] In other words, soft landings are possible.

Chapter 4

Good Riddance to Empire, Part 1: Arrogance and Interests

And if a sparrow cannot fall to the ground without His notice, is it probable that an Empire can rise without His aid?
—LYNNE AND DICK CHENEY'S CHRISTMAS CARD, DECEMBER 2003[1]

Yet what word but "empire" describes the awesome thing that America is becoming? It is the only nation that polices the world through five global military commands; maintains more than a million men and women at arms on four continents; deploys carrier battle groups on watch in every ocean; guarantees the survival of countries from Israel to South Korea; drives the wheels of global trade and commerce; and fills the hearts and minds of an entire planet with its dreams and desires. —MICHAEL IGNATIEFF[2]

The Department of Defense is not, today, a department of defense. It's an alternative seat of government on the south bank of the Potomac River. And typical of militarism, it's expanding into many, many other areas in our life that we have, in our traditional political philosophy, reserved for civilians. —CHALMERS JOHNSON[3]

INTRODUCTION

We have entered a historical period in which U.S. living standards have deteriorated significantly and U.S. wars have gone badly. In light of present difficulties it may be hard to remember the grandiose arrogance that marked the rhetoric and ambition of U.S. leaders as the Cold War ended with the dissolution of the Soviet Union in 1991. It was common wisdom among Republicans, Democrats, and many citizens that the United States "won" the Cold War. Victory confirmed America's moral superiority, economic strength, and military supremacy. Some leaders and commentators spoke openly about American empire. America's rise was part of God's plan and American exceptionalism and militarism were celebrated. Others, like political economist Francis Fukuyama, went even further, writing glowingly about the end of history: "What we may be witnessing is not just the end of the Cold War or the passing of a particular period of post-war history, but the end of history as such: that is, the end point of mankind's ideological evolution and the universalization of Western liberal democracy as the final form of human government."[4]

The neoconservative foreign policy experts that rose to prominence in the administrations of George W. Bush were eager to reshape the world in their image through the aggressive use of U.S. military power. They believed that under their leadership a dangerous world could be transformed and American supremacy made permanent. Linking so-called American ideals to the aggressive application of military force, they set out to dominate the world by implementing what they called "America's grand strategy."

Practical elements of a grand strategy surfaced in a Defense Planning Guidance (DPG) draft written in 1992 by Paul Wolfowitz on behalf of Defense Secretary Dick Cheney. The DPG draft laid out guidelines for reshaping U.S. foreign policies now that U.S. power was no longer constrained by the Soviet Union. Wolfowitz became Donald Rumsfeld's deputy secretary of defense during the Bush administration and along with Vice President Cheney was well positioned to put their ideas into practice. "Our first objective is to prevent the re-emergence of a new rival," the DPG draft stated. "This is a dominant consideration . . . and requires that we endeavor to prevent any hostile power from dominating a region whose resources would, under consolidated control, be sufficient to generate global power." No nation or group of nations would be allowed to seriously challenge U.S. power, especially control of Middle Eastern oil. In fact, no rival would be tolerated anywhere, not in "Western Europe, East Asia, the territory of the former Soviet Union, [or] Southwest Asia." The "first objective" of U.S. foreign policy was to "maintain the mechanisms for deterring potential competitors from even aspiring to a larger regional or global role."

No nation was in a position to stop the United States, and so the DPG draft advocated aggressive use of military power worldwide to secure its advantages. This would allow the United States to make its dominant position permanent, "spread democratic forms of government and open economic systems," counter regional threats such as Iraq and North Korea, and secure "access to vital raw materials, primarily Persian Gulf oil."

The DPG draft also emphasized unilateralism. In order to turn present military advantages into permanent global supremacy the United States needed to be free of constraints imposed by international agreements and laws. There was no mention of taking collective action through the United Nations. The United States "should expect future coalitions to be ad hoc assemblies" to deal with particular crises. It "should be postured to act independently when collective action cannot be orchestrated."[5]

As we will see, the goals and ambitions evident in the DPG draft were later embodied in a grand strategy that included the invasion of Iraq. Not surprisingly, hubristic values and actions delivered the polar opposites of promised results. America's economic, ecological, and military crises offer cautionary tales. When we allow ourselves to be seduced by comforting myths of American exceptionalism, we endanger ourselves and others. When we allow groups that benefit from war and excessive military spending to seek global domination while claiming to spread lofty ideals and to defend the nation, we undermine authentic security. In opposition to the Cheney's post-Iraq-invasion Christmas-card claim, American empire is not part of God's master plan. The pursuit of militarized empire is guided by human arrogance, not divine will. It is costly in lives and treasure, causing untold suffering, exposing the nation to unnecessary danger, and accelerating the pace of U.S. economic and moral decline.

The conscious rejection of American exceptionalism and saying good riddance to empire are keys to authentic hope and security. Soft landings are possible, but two self-serving ideas must die a timely death: the widespread view that the United States has a unique mission that both allows and requires it to project military power worldwide, and the unwarranted belief in the usefulness of military power. Together they encourage aggressive intervention in the affairs of other nations, a bloated national security establishment, and a war culture that presumes both are necessary to keep us safe. Many Americans were upset by aggressive embodiment of these ideas in the foreign policies of George W. Bush, but his rhetoric, values, and policies were in basic continuity with those of past and present administrations. These ideas and values are reinforced consistently by U.S. presidents, politicians from each major political party, the media, and popular culture.

Empires sow the seeds of their own collapse. In this chapter I describe signs of stress that befall all would-be empires, including the United States, as they enter a period of decline. I demonstrate that the post–Cold War period was a time of increased militarism and national arrogance as U.S. leaders internalized views of American exceptionalism and aspired openly to empire. They misread history, overestimated the usefulness of military power, ignored countervailing signs, and set out to dominate the world. Unfortunately, despite recent setbacks they still do. I also make the case that present wars, military spending levels, and foreign policies are not really intended to keep us safe. They satisfy the power and profit imperatives of entrenched groups and project power globally in defense of "interests," a vague category that obscures real goals and intentions. The U.S. national security establishment, far from defending the country, morphed to become the greatest threat to our nation's well-being.

This chapter sets the stage for chapter 5, which describes many economic and social benefits of saying good riddance to empire and lays out pathways to soft landings, including alternative foreign policies that would improve U.S. security and quality of life. It's the end of the world as we know it in terms of arrogant ambitions and aggressive foreign policies. This is very good news indeed. Saying good riddance to empire gives us a realistic chance for soft landings, including opportunities to build a more equitable, sustainable economy and to address climate change.

A POLITICS OF FEAR

American leaders have long presumed that the United States has the moral authority, economic capacity, and military means to dominate global affairs. This attitude may be common to all aspiring empires, but it reflects arrogance that contributes inevitably to a nation's decline. There are four clear signs of trouble for would-be empires, including our own. The first is that politics becomes dominated by fear, which is used to justify militarization and galvanize support for war. "Keep elevating the threat," Secretary of Defense Donald Rumsfeld urged his subordinates following 9/11. "Make the American people realize they are surrounded in the world by violent extremists."[6] Herman Goering, Hitler's heir apparent, understood well the power of fear. While imprisoned at Nuremberg, he told the prison psychologist:

> Naturally, the common people don't want war, neither in Russia, nor England, nor for that matter, Germany. That is understood, but after all it is the leaders of the country who determine the policy and it is always a simple matter to drag the people along, whether it is a democracy, or fascist dictatorship, or a parliament, or a communist dictatorship. Voice or no voice, the people can always be brought to the bidding of the leaders. That is easy. All you have to do is tell them they are being attacked, and denounce the peacemakers for

lack of patriotism and exposing the country to danger. It works the same in any country.[7]

GOOD VERSUS EVIL

A second sign of imperial stress is that yarns are spun in which enemies are cast as barbarous villains and the nation as virtuous savior even as one's own conduct undermines claims of moral authority. "Certain of our own benign intentions," Andrew Bacevich writes, "we reflexively assign responsibility for war to others, typically malignant Hitler-like figures inexplicably bent on denying us the peace that is our fondest wish." "The enemy of humility is sanctimony," he writes, "which gives rise to the conviction that American values and beliefs are universal and that the nation itself serves providentially assigned purposes."[8]

U.S. presidents and politicians have often claimed moral authority to justify militarization and aggressive foreign policies that would be condemned if carried out by any other nation. George W. Bush offered a virtual litany of sanctimonious claims in his presidential speeches. "The advance of freedom is more than an interest we pursue. It is a calling we follow. . . . America seeks to expand, not the borders of our country, but the realm of liberty."[9] "Our responsibility to history is already clear, to answer these attacks and rid the world of evil."[10] "Our nation's cause has always been larger than our nation's defense. We fight, as we always fight, for a just peace—a peace that favors liberty."[11] "Our country is strong. And our cause is even larger than our country. Ours is the cause of human dignity; freedom guided by conscience and guarded by peace. This ideal of America is the hope of all mankind."[12]

As Bacevich writes, "Bush was simply putting his own gloss on a time-honored conviction ascribing to the United States a uniqueness of character . . . [that serves a] providential purpose. Paying homage to, and therefore renewing, this tradition of American exceptionalism has long been one of the presidency's primary extraconstitutional obligations."[13]

The tradition continues. "I still believe that America is the last, best hope of Earth," Senator Barack Obama said in his first major campaign speech addressing foreign policy. "We must lead by building a twenty-first century military to ensure the security of our people and advance the security of all people." "The American moment has not passed. The American moment is here. And like generations before us, we will seize that moment, and begin the world anew."[14]

Ironically, President Obama, who increased military spending, expanded foreign wars, extended presidential powers, and embraced many ideas and policies of his predecessor has been criticized harshly for not sufficiently championing American exceptionalism. "This reorientation away from a celebration of American exceptionalism is misguided and bankrupt," former Massachusetts governor Mitt Romney wrote in the context of pushing forth his presidential bid. A chapter in Sarah Palin's recent book is titled "America the Exceptional." Former House Speaker Newt Gingrich called President Obama's views on American exceptionalism "truly alarming," and former Arkansas governor Mike Huckabee criticized the president saying that to "deny American exceptionalism is in essence to deny the heart and soul of this nation."[15]

Other conservative commentators defended the president. For example, after a speech in which President Obama justified U.S. intervention in Libya, Bill Kristol of the *Weekly Standard* said that with this speech the "President Obama had rejoined—or joined—the historical American foreign policy mainstream" and "the president was unapologetic, freedom-agenda-embracing, and didn't shrink from defending the use of force or from appealing to American values and interests." And Steve Benen wrote approvingly that in Obama's speech "the president wasn't subtle—the United States isn't like other countries; ours is a country with unique power, responsibilities, and moral obligations."[16] Glen Greenwald provided an apt summary of this false debate. "It's long been obvious that Obama deeply believes in American exceptionalism . . . " He went on to describe the salient point:

The fact remains that declaring yourself special, superior and/or exceptional—and believing that to be true, and, especially, acting on that belief—has serious consequences. It can (and usually does) mean that the same standards of judgment aren't applied to your acts as are applied to everyone else's (when you do X, it's justified, but when they do, it isn't). It means that you're entitled (or obligated) to do things that nobody else is entitled or obligated to do. . . . It means that no matter how many bad things you do in the world, it doesn't ever reflect on *who you are*, because you're *inherently* exceptional and thus driven by good motives. And it probably means—at least as it expresses itself in the American form—that you'll find yourself in a posture of endless war, because your "unique power, responsibilities, and moral obligations" will always find causes and justifications for new conflicts.[17]

Framing global conflicts in terms of good versus evil and your nation's special calling may temporarily help galvanize people for war, but it conceals more than it reveals. Similarly, claims of U.S. moral superiority and special mission often blind us to the immorality of our nation's actions that others see clearly. These include decades of U.S. support for repressive dictators in Latin America and much of the so-called Third World, U.S. invasions and occupations of other countries for oil, efforts to block or weaken international climate treaties, widespread use of torture, and an array of other inconsistencies. As Benjamin Barber wrote in *Fear's Empire*, "American autonomy, American virtue, American democracy, and American innocence—are reasserted with patriotic ardor at home, even as they are deemed hollow and hypocritical abroad."[18]

American exceptionalism feeds militarism and is fed by uncritical patriotism, including idealization of the troops. "If you're looking for a clear sign of a militarized society—which few Americans are—a good place to start is with troop veneration," writes William Astore.[19] "Ever since the events of 9/11, there's been an almost religious veneration of U.S. service members." The problem with "elevating our troops to hero status" is that "we often forget that war is guaranteed to degrade humanity" and "we ensure that the brutalizing aspects and effects of war will be played down." He notes that when "we create a legion of heroes in our minds, we blind ourselves to evidence of their destructive, sometimes atrocious behavior. By making our military generically heroic, we act to prolong our wars."[20] He is particularly troubled by cheap cultural expressions of patriotism:

> I'm tired of seeing simpleminded magnetic ribbons on vehicles telling me, a 20-year veteran, to support or pray for our troops. As a Christian, I find it presumptuous to see ribbons shaped like fish, with an American flag as a tail, informing me that God blesses our troops. I'm underwhelmed by gigantic American flags—up to 100 feet by 300 feet—repeatedly being unfurled in our sports arenas, as if our love of country is greater when our flags are bigger. I'm disturbed by nuclear-strike bombers soaring over stadiums filled with children, as one did in July just as the National Anthem ended during this year's Major League Baseball All Star game. Instead of oohing and aahing at our destructive might, I was quietly horrified at its looming presence during a family event. . . . We as a country have yet to face, no less curtail, our ongoing steroidal celebrations of pumped-up patriotism.[21]

Claims of "American innocence" and of American exceptionalism limit our capacity to understand the world we live in. Americans have little knowledge of the motivation and actual impact of U.S. foreign policies. My wife and I lived in Central America in the 1980s, when the United States backed repressive groups and governments throughout the region, including death squads in El Salvador and Guatemala and a brutal insurgency in Nicaragua. The CIA had produced a manual for the Nicaraguan contras on how to maximize the political and psychological impact of terrorism, including instruction on political assassinations and slitting throats.[22] We met many European aid and development workers during this time who told us they considered Americans the best-educated ignorant people on the planet because we are woefully unaware of the motivation and impact of many U.S. foreign policies.

Americans have a hard time understanding why the United States is disliked by many people throughout the world. We seem genuinely baffled about why a group like al Qaeda would want to harm us by carrying out terrorist attacks against U.S. targets. Clyde Prestowitz, a former official in the Reagan administration, wrote that we attribute "criticism of American policies to envy of our success and power and to chronic anti-Americanism. . . . Perhaps we should also look at how we deal with some key issues and how our behavior is perceived and comports with our values."[23]

Americans have almost no context within which to make sense of conflicts that seem to emerge out of thin air. In this we are aided by a complicit media that consistently reinforces the myth of American exceptionalism. It's as if we seek to understand complex matters and our own confusion by picking up a 500-page book and beginning to read on page 497. Without context, it is difficult to connect disturbing events that conflict with an idealized portrait of the United States with troubling U.S. foreign policies we know little about. Chalmers Johnson refers to this as blowback. "By blowback we do not mean just the unintended consequences of events [U.S. foreign policies]. We mean unintended consequences of events that were kept secret from the American public, so that when the retaliation comes, the public has no way to put it into context."[24]

U.S. history in Afghanistan offers a clear example of blowback. Most Americans are unaware that radical Muslims who carried out the devastating terrorist attacks on September 11, 2001, were former allies of the United States and that many had been the beneficiaries of billions of dollars in U.S. support, training, and weapons. Many radical Muslims (the Mujahadeen), including Osama bin Laden, later morphed into al Qaeda. The official history of this period says that the United States began aiding the Mujahadeen in response to the Soviet Union's invasion of Afghanistan in 1979. The official story is a lie. Former CIA director Robert Gates (later President Obama's secretary of defense) states in his memoirs that American intelligence services began aiding the Mujahadeen six months *before* the Soviet invasion. Zbigniew Brzezinski, national security advisor to President Jimmy Carter, stated the U.S. intent: "we knowingly increased the probability" of a Soviet invasion. He told the president, "We now have the opportunity of giving to the USSR its Vietnam War." Brzezinski was asked in a 1998 interview if he regretted this policy. He responded: "Regret what? It had the effect of drawing the Russians into the Afghan trap." The interviewer tried one more time:

> *Interviewer*: "And neither do you regret having supported Islamic fundamentalism, having given arms and advice to future terrorists?"

> *Brzezinski*: "What is most important to the history of the world? The Taliban or the collapse of the Soviet Union? Some stirred-up Moslems or the liberation of Central Europe and the end of the Cold War?"[25]

Our socialization allows blowback to catch us unaware. Empires seem to have an ironclad unwritten rule that protects them from scrutinizing their claims of moral superiority. On very, very rare occasions a mistake can be acknowledged, but never can a series of "mistakes" be linked together to reveal deeper character flaws. As Robert Scheer writes: "Americans who blithely claim the moral high ground with every pledge of allegiance to a flag that, because it is American, is assumed to have never been sullied by imperial greed or moral contradiction expect no less than instant and full forgiveness for our 'mistakes.'"[26]

POWER PROJECTION
AND DEFENSE OF "INTERESTS"

A third sign of imperial stress is that the national security establishment in a faltering empire sacrifices defense of the nation and the safety of its citizens to goals of projecting global power to protect "interests." The disastrous implications of this strategy should be clear in light of the terror attacks of September 11, 2001. As Bacevich notes, a "political elite preoccupied with the governance of empire paid little attention to protecting the United States itself. . . . The institution nominally referred to as the Department of Defense didn't actually do defense; it specialized in power projection." This may seem odd but when "it came to defending vital American interests, asserting control over the imperial periphery took precedence over guarding the nation's own perimeter."[27]

Let me illustrate this sign of imperial crisis with an analogy that distinguishes between authentic security and protection of interests. In Scenario One people and leaders in my country take steps to keep families, homes, neighborhoods, and nation safe and secure. We live modestly and within our means both as families and as a nation so as not to increase vulnerability during an unforeseen crisis. We build relationships of friendship and trust within and reach out to people and leaders of other nations to deepen cultural understanding and economic ties. Knowing that nations with higher degrees of equity have less crime, violence, and other social problems, we elect leaders who support quality schools and public policies that distribute widely the benefits of the economy. We work to establish an agreed-upon set of laws delineating our rights and responsibilities as citizens. Similar rules guide interactions and relations between our nation and other countries. When conflicts arise within or without they are adjudicated by a fair judicial system or within a system of international treaties and laws. Some citizens choose to side with caution and fence in their yards, purchase guard dogs, or install home security systems. Most happily pay for adequate police and fire services and for a modest military with sufficient means to deter would-be aggressors. There is no such thing as absolute security, but our families, homes, neighborhoods, and nation are relatively safe and secure.

This approach contrasts sharply with another that focuses on protecting interests, not safety or security. In Scenario Two leaders in my country are not satisfied with the modest scenario depicted above. The nation has become wealthy and powerful, privileged compared to other countries. Leaders are ambitious and generally represent the interests of the wealthy. They believe that the nation's good fortune is a sign of God's favor and that our nation has special rights and responsibilities to spread influence and expand privileges. It also has lots of wants and needs. Houses are huge, and fleets of gas-guzzling cars require lots of oil that our nation can't supply.

It turns out that a distant nation has lots of oil. Our leaders want that oil and oil from other distant countries in order to increase consumption even though our own oil reserves have fallen dramatically and we could take steps to reduce consumption. We now have interests. Unfortunately, some leaders of these distant nations aren't very cooperative. Although they in no way threaten the safety of our families, homes, neighborhoods, or nation, they imperil our way of life. They threaten our interests.

There are rules that almost every other nation must follow, but because my country is exceptional and powerful, our leaders ignore them. We pull some strings and have uncooperative foreign leaders overthrown and replaced by those who respect our wishes. They are willing to do pretty much whatever we say and are well compensated. We now have common interests. Our relationship deepens, which is important because in order to help us, they can't be very good to their own citizens. This breeds a good deal of resentment because these leaders seem much more concerned with the wishes of our leaders than the needs of their own people. We give military training to them and their friends and supply them with weapons. This keeps them in power and protects our interests. When this proves inadequate we send our troops to be stationed permanently in their country. Our troops are sometimes attacked by people who threaten our interests. We call them insurgents or terrorists. Pretty soon we've trained foreign troops and built military bases housing our soldiers in countries all over the world to defend our interests.

It may not be a perfect analogy but you get the point. Militarism is not defense. Defending interests isn't the same thing as defending legitimate security needs. Faltering empires see their "interests" being challenged everywhere and militarism as the appropriate response. The implication for empires, including our own, is clear from this description of imperial Rome by historian Joseph Schumpeter:

> There was no corner of the known world where some interest was not alleged to be in danger or under actual attack. If the interests were not Roman, they were those of Rome's allies; and if Rome had no allies, then allies would be invented. When it was utterly impossible to contrive such an interest—why, then it was the national honor that had been insulted. The fight was always invested with an aura of legality. Rome was always being attacked by evil-minded neighbors, always fighting for a breathing space. The whole world was pervaded by a host of enemies, and it was manifestly Rome's duty to guard against their indubitably aggressive designs. They were enemies who only waited to fall on the Roman people.[28]

ECONOMIC CONSEQUENCES OF MILITARISM

The fourth sign of imperial stress is when increased militarization causes economic difficulties and social decline. A faltering empire inevitably reaches a point when excessive and increasingly counterproductive use of military power contrasts sharply with, and contributes mightily to, diminished economic capacity. French historian Emmanuel Todd recognized this dynamic in the Soviet Union and rightly predicted its rapid fall. He saw this pattern repeating itself in the United States at the very time U.S. national arrogance and imperial ambition reached its zenith.

Todd, writing just months after the invasion of Iraq, said that for the United States, like the Soviet Union, the "expansion of military activity" was seen "as a sign of increasing power when in fact it serves to mask a decline."[29] "America no longer has the economic and financial resources to back up its foreign policy objectives." Huge trade deficits with the rest of the world signal that "financially speaking America has become the planet's glorious beggar." It has become the chief "predator of the globalized economy." Its "dramatic militarization" has made it "a superpower that is economically dependent but also politically useless."[30] According to Todd, "this America—militaristic, agitated, uncertain, anxious country projecting its own disorder around the globe—is hardly the 'indispensable nation' it claims to be and is certainly not what the rest of the world really needs now."[31] The United States was working hard "to maintain the illusory fiction of the world as a dangerous place in need of America's protection." "The exaggeration of the Iraqi threat," he said, "will be remembered as only the first act in America's dramatic staging of nonexistent global dangers that the United States will rush to save us from." This folly would inevitably "provoke a radical weakening of its position in the world in the near future."[32]

Todd's warnings were ignored and would have seemed ludicrous to many. A flurry of imperial praise was heaped on the body politic from commentators from Right to Left after the fall of Baghdad. The rhetoric, impressive by any standard, was even more startling given that subsequent events exposed its delusions. Architects of the war David Frum and Richard Perle declared Operation Iraqi Freedom "a vivid and compelling demonstration of America's ability to win swift and total victory." Neocon Max Boot said the war proved that U.S. military excellence "far surpasses the capabilities of such previous would-be-hegemons as Rome, Britain, and Napoleonic France." U.S. forces demonstrated "unparalleled strength in every facet of warfare" to the point that we "just don't need anyone else's help very much." And the commander of U.S. forces, General Tommy Franks, claimed that his effort was "unequalled in its

excellence by anything in the annals of war."[33] *New York Times* colum-
nist Thomas Friedman (I'm not sure where he fits on a political spec-
trum) gushed that "this war is the most important liberal, revolutionary
U.S. democracy-building project since the Marshall Plan." He lauded
the war as "one of the noblest things this country has ever attempted
abroad."[34] And writing from the left at about the same time Michael
Ignatieff praised the rise of America's empire.[35]

Emmanuel Todd, it should be noted, is a friend of the United States,
but friends don't let friends drive drunk. The basic facts of our predicament and the trajectory of where we are headed are clear. Excessive
militarization is undermining authentic security and accelerating the
pace of internal decline. To avoid a rapid fall and to have any realistic chance of soft landings we need a radical course correction soon.
Ironically, assigning god-like qualities to militarism weakens both the
nation's economy and its military capacity. Immanuel Wallerstein wrote
in 2003 that the invasion of Iraq "far from validating and increasing the
military power of the United States, will undermine it grievously in the
short, middle, and long run."[36] "A soft landing for America forty years
from now? Don't bet on it. The demise of the United States as the global
superpower could come far more quickly than anyone imagines," writes
University of Wisconsin Professor of History Alfred McCoy. "If Washington is dreaming of 2040 or 2050 as the end of the American Century,
a more realistic assessment of domestic and global trends suggests that
in 2025 . . . it could all be over except the shouting."[37]

DANGEROUS DELUSIONS:
MISREADING HISTORY

The end of the Cold War was greeted in the United States with a large
measure of triumphalism. Advocates of more aggressive foreign policies convinced themselves that the United States had a special mission
and unique opportunity to expand U.S. influence, reshape the world,

dominate global affairs, and access a disproportionate share of global resources through an ambitious use and display of military power. Their core ideas, expressed in the DPG draft described earlier, evolved further within conservative think tanks such as The Project for the New American Century (PNAC).[38] Of particular relevance was PNAC's report "Rebuilding America's Defenses" (RAD), which was published a year before the terrorist attacks of September 11, 2001.[39] RAD was a detailed plan to achieve global domination through the unilateral use of military force. "The Defense Policy Guidance (DPG) drafted in the early months of 1992 provided a blueprint for maintaining preeminence, precluding the rise of a great power rival, and shaping the international security order in line with American principles and interests," the authors of RAD wrote. The "basic tenets of the DPG, in our judgment, remain sound."

RAD reiterated that no nation or group of nations could constrain U.S. power. "The Cold War world was a bipolar world; the 21st century is—for the moment, at least—decidedly unipolar, with America as the world's 'sole superpower.'" "At no time in history has the international security order been as conducive to American interests and ideals. The challenge for the coming century is to preserve and enhance this 'American peace.'" The fundamental premise was "that U.S. military capabilities should be sufficient to support *an American grand strategy* committed to building upon this unprecedented opportunity." "America's grand strategy should aim to preserve and extend this advantageous position as far into the future as possible."

Increase Military Spending

The authors of RAD believed permanent global domination could be achieved with significant increases in military spending. This was a striking recommendation given that the Soviet Union no longer existed and the United States had no serious challengers. Although at "present the United States faced no global rival . . . even a global *Pax Americana* will not preserve itself." "Unless the United States maintains sufficient military strength, this opportunity will be lost." "Preserving the desirable strategic situation in which the United States now finds itself requires a globally preeminent military capability both today and in the future." The U.S. military needed additional resources to "fight and decisively win multiple, simultaneous major theater wars," "perform the 'constabulary' duties associated with shaping the security environment in critical regions," "maintain nuclear strategic superiority," "develop and deploy global missile defenses," and "insure the long-term superiority of U.S. conventional forces." With sufficient funds it would be possible "to maintain the United States as the 'arsenal of democracy' for the 21st century."

Regime Change

America's grand strategy included regime change in Iraq as part of broader commitments to wage preventive wars. RAD shifted U.S. strategic doctrine further in the direction of offensive war. "Today . . . security can only be acquired at the 'retail' level by deterring or, when needed, by compelling regional foes to act in ways that protect American interests and principles." It criticized prior "Pentagon war games" for having "given little or no consideration to the force requirements necessary . . . to remove these regimes [North Korea, Iraq] from power." RAD declared the right of the United States to attack others when its interests were threatened or might be threatened in the future. It "is important to shape circumstances before crises emerge, and to meet threats before they become dire."

Oil and Bases

RAD's authors called on U.S. leaders to take additional steps to control the world's oil supplies and to put permanent military bases in the Middle East. These goals were closely linked. Controlling oil supplies required a military presence in the Middle East and elsewhere. They also converged with the goal of regime change because Iraq held the second or third largest oil reserves in the world and was a potential site for permanent U.S. bases. "Ever since World War II, when American policymakers first acknowledged that the United States would someday become dependent on Middle Eastern petroleum, it has been American policy to ensure that the United States would always have unrestrained access to Persian Gulf oil," Michael Klare wrote just prior to the U.S. invasion of Iraq. This policy led the United States to back repressive autocratic governments in the region. When the strategy faltered with the overthrow of the Shah of Iran in 1979, President Jimmy Carter announced the Carter Doctrine. It "states that unrestricted access to the Persian Gulf is a vital interest of the United States and that, in protection of that interest, the United States will employ 'any means necessary, including military force.' "[40]

A major U.S. objective during the first Gulf War (1991) was to establish a permanent military ground presence in the oil-rich region, including in Saudi Arabia. The U.S. success in doing so led Osama bin Laden to orchestrate terror attacks against U.S. targets. RAD, written a year before 9/11, reported a "geometric increase in the presence of U.S. armed forces" in the "Persian Gulf and surrounding region" since the end of the Cold War. "Indeed, the United States has for decades sought to play a more permanent role in Gulf regional security. While the unresolved conflict with Iraq provides the immediate justification, the need for a substantial American force presence in the Gulf transcends the issue of the regime of Saddam Hussein."

The presence of U.S. forces and semipermanent bases near the holiest sites of Islam created problems for governments in the region because it fueled popular resentments. The "Air Force presence in the Gulf region is a vital one for U.S. military strategy, and the United States should consider it a de facto permanent presence, even as it seeks ways to lessen Saudi, Kuwaiti and regional concerns about the U.S. presence." Despite popular resentment and an increased likelihood of terrorism, RAD recommended that "a permanent unit" of the U.S. Army "be based in the Persian Gulf Region."

Expansion of Capabilities and the Use of Military Power to Achieve RAD Objectives

America's grand strategy highlighted the need to improve U.S. intervention capabilities and increase dramatically the actual use of U.S. military force to achieve key objectives. This required a significant expansion of the U.S. military footprint, including additional foreign bases and a willingness to invade and occupy other nations. The "presence of American forces in critical regions around the world is the visible expression of America's status as a superpower." The United States needed to carry out numerous "constabulary missions," a euphemism for global sheriff duties that were self-appointed.

Unilateralism

RAD displays an almost god-like faith in U.S. military power to achieve strategic objectives. Its authors recognized, however, that U.S. intervention and preventive wars wouldn't be accepted by the international community. This led them to emphasize unilateralism as part of their grand strategy. U.S. "constabulary missions, are far more complex and likely to generate violence than traditional 'peacekeeping' missions," and they demanded "American political leadership rather than that of the United Nations," which was ineffective. "Nor can the United States assume a UN-like stance of neutrality; the preponderance of American power is so great and its global interests so wide that it cannot pretend to be indifferent to the political outcome" in the Persian Gulf and elsewhere.

"Missile Defense"

The grand strategy also called for development and deployment of a missile defense system in order to enhance U.S. intervention capabilities. Missile defense is usually presented as, well, defensive. We need to protect ourselves from nasty state and nonstate actors who irrationally want to harm us. RAD is more honest about U.S. intentions. Missile defense would "provide a secure basis for U.S. power projection around the world" so that the United States could intervene anywhere without fear of reprisal. It was to be "the central element in the exercise of American power and the projection of U.S. military forces abroad. Without it weak states operating small arsenals of crude ballistic missiles, armed with basic nuclear warheads or other weapons of mass destruction, will be . . . in a strong position to deter the United States from using conventional force. . . . America's ability to project power will be deeply compromised." "The failure to build missile defenses" would "compromise the exercise of American power abroad" which would "ensure that the current *Pax Americana* comes to an early end."

Nuclear Strategic Superiority

The grand strategy committed the United States to "maintain nuclear strategic superiority." RAD says four things concerning nuclear weapons. First, adversaries seek nuclear or chemical weapons to deter the United States from invading or destroying them through conventional warfare. Second, this is an effective strategy that could place dangerous limits on "the exercise of American power abroad." Third, the United States should "remove . . . regimes from power" that have or seek such a deterrent. Finally, in a classic example of double standards, the United States should develop and deploy a new generation of useable nukes.

The Bush administration submitted its Nuclear Posture Review (NPR) to Congress in December 2001, which targeted a broad range of potential adversaries for nuclear attack, including China, Iran, Iraq, Russia, Syria, North Korea, and Libya. It called for development of "nuclear offensive forces" as part of a "capabilities approach" to nuclear weapons and raised the possibility of development of a new generation of lower-yield systems. It also raised the specter of nuclear weapons deployed in space as part of a multi-tiered missile defense system.[41]

Militarization of Space

Although the United States had previously written and signed a UN treaty to keep space for peaceful purposes, a central component in America's grand strategy was militarization of space. RAD acknowledged that "American landpower remains the essential link in the chain that translates U.S. military supremacy into American geopolitical preeminence" and that "the increasing sophistication of American air power" allows it to "attack any target on earth with great accuracy and virtual impunity." Militarization of space, however, was seen as the key to achieving military supremacy and permanent global domination.

RAD stated that "maintaining control of space will inevitably require the application of force both in space and from space, including but not limited to antimissile defenses and defensive systems capable of protecting U.S. and allied satellites; space control cannot be sustained in any other fashion." It said "space dominance may become so essential to the preservation of American military preeminence that it may require a separate service." In order for "U.S. armed forces to continue to assert military preeminence, control of space—defined by Space Command as 'the ability to assure access to space, freedom of operations within the space medium, and an ability to deny others the use of space'—must be an essential element of our military strategy." RAD warned that if the United States "cannot maintain that control, its ability to conduct global military operations will be severely complicated, far more costly, and potentially fatally compromised." U.S. efforts to militarize space are ongoing. In October 2006 the UN General Assembly approved a resolution to prevent an arms race in space by a vote of 166 to 1 with the United States casting the lone no vote.[42]

OPPORTUNITY LOST?

The problem facing the authors of RAD wasn't that "America's grand strategy" was blatantly imperial, although it was. Their strategy was built on the foundations of previous foreign policies and was consistent with ideological claims of American exceptionalism that had dominated our national narrative for generations. The problem was much simpler: Their grand strategy was likely to be ignored because the costs of implementation were considered prohibitive even by ardent militarists who had influenced U.S. military strategies for generations. Imagine the frustration and disappointment of RAD's authors. They saw a unique moment in history ripe with opportunities. They developed a detailed plan that they believed could be implemented under their direction to achieve permanent global domination. And yet it was unlikely to see the light of day because it was too expensive. The U.S. people wouldn't be willing to pay the enormous costs in lives and treasure unless they could be galvanized by a traumatic event. Writing a year before 9/11, the authors of RAD put it this way: "the process of transformation, even if it brings revolutionary changes, is likely to be a long one, *absent some catastrophic and catalyzing event—like a new Pearl Harbor.*"

The previous sentence has given rise to conspiracy theories suggesting that the terror attacks were an inside job. Conspiracies are hard to prove, however, and what we know for certain is damaging enough. Members of the Bush administration, many of them RAD signatories, treated 9/11 as their new Pearl Harbor. "For the Bush administration, September 11 was a bonanza for its preexisting agenda," writes Immanuel Wallerstein.[43] They actively cultivated a politics of fear and took advantage of the nation's trauma. And they jump-started implementation of their grand strategy with the invasion of Iraq. They did so with support from Democrats and Republicans based on manufactured intelligence. General Anthony Zinni said it this way:

We had to create a false rationale for going in [to Iraq] to get public support. The books were cooked, in my mind. The intelligence was not there. I testified before the Senate Foreign Relations Committee one month before the war, and Senator Lugar asked me: "General Zinni, do you feel the threat from Saddam Hussein is imminent?" I said: "No, not at all. It was not an imminent threat. Not even close. Not grave, gathering, imminent, serious, severe, mildly upsetting, none of those.[44]

Each component of America's grand strategy was pushed forward or became official policy with publication of the Bush administration's report on the National Security Strategy of the United States (NSS) in September 2002. The NSS report also heaped contempt on the International Criminal Court (ICC). The NSS stated: "We will take the actions necessary to ensure that our efforts to meet our global security commitments and protect Americans are not impaired by the potential investigations, inquiry, or prosecution by the International Criminal Court (ICC), whose jurisdiction does not extend to Americans and which we do not accept."[45] The NSS expressed the U.S. government's determination to "implement fully the American Servicemembers Protection Act, whose provisions are intended to ensure and enhance the protection of U.S. personnel and officials."[46] This act stated: "Members of the Armed Forces of the United States should be free from the risk of prosecution by the International Criminal Court, especially when they are stationed or deployed around the world to protect the vital national interests of the United States."[47] Human Rights Watch called it the "Hague Invasion Act." The law "is intended to intimidate countries that ratify the treaty for the International Criminal Court (ICC). The new law *authorizes the use of military force to liberate any American citizen or a U.S. allied country being held by the court*, which is located in The Hague." It also provides for "the withdrawal of U.S. military assistance from countries ratifying the ICC treaty and restricts U.S. participation in United Nations peacekeeping unless the United States obtains immunity from prosecution."[48]

"WE'RE AN EMPIRE NOW"

Ron Suskind, a *Wall Street Journal* reporter, captured a moment that crystallized the arrogance of U.S. leaders following 9/11. Shortly before the U.S. invasion of Iraq, he met with a high-level official in the Bush administration (widely believed to be Karl Rove). Suskind shared his view that the invasion would likely have disastrous consequences for both Iraq and the United States. He describes the response he received this way:

> The aide said that guys like me were "in what we call the reality-based community," which he defined as people who "believe that solutions emerge from your judicious study of discernible reality. . . . That's not the way the world really works anymore," he continued. "*We're an empire now, and when we act, we create our own reality.* And while you're studying that reality—judiciously, as you will—we'll act again, creating other new realities, which you can study too, and that's how things will sort out. We're history's actors . . . and you, all of you, will be left to just study what we do."[49]

Raw ambition combined with effusive and delusional rhetoric led psychologist Robert Jay Lifton to diagnose the United States as suffering from "superpower syndrome" which he defined as "a national mindset—put forward strongly by a tight-knit leadership group—that takes on a sense of omnipotence, of unique standing in the world that grants it the right to hold sway over all other nations." "Any such project . . . becomes enmeshed in fantasy, in dreams of imposing an omnipotent will on others, and in the urge to control history itself," Lifton writes. "Driven by superpower syndrome, such visions of domination and control can prove catastrophic when, as they must, they come up against the irredeemable stubbornness of reality.[50]

The custodians of empire were determined to implement "America's grand strategy." The terror attacks allowed them to proceed. They doubled U.S. military spending. They violated international laws, ignored the Geneva conventions, and abused the United Nations. They redefined torture and opposed protocols prescribing torture. They established preventive war as official doctrine and conducted "constabulary missions" to control oil and defend other interests. This inevitably involved U.S. leaders and soldiers in serious breaches of international law and so they sought to undermine the ICC. They also shredded the constitution expanded presidential powers, and violated civil liberties. By objective standards of "the reality-based community," they should have been subject to and accountable for crimes against humanity, genocide, or crimes of war as defined by the Nuremburg Principles, the Geneva Conventions, and the 1984 Convention against Torture. We have not only been left to study what they did but to try to deal with the disastrous consequences of their delusions, which unfortunately are not unique among our nation's leaders and foreign policy planners.

CONTINUITY

U.S. leaders have long claimed a unique right for themselves and the nation to stand above international laws and norms.[51] For many decades militarism has been an elephant in the room of which few are willing to speak, and the elephant is exceptionally well fed no matter who inhabits the White House. I am sixty years old and cannot remember a time when the United States wasn't engaged in overt or covert warfare. As Glen Greenwald writes:

> There was a time, not all that long ago, when the U.S. pretended that it viewed war only as a last resort, something to be used only when absolutely necessary to defend the country against imminent threats. In reality, at least since the creation of the National Security State in the wake of World War II, war for the U.S. has been everything but a "last resort." Constant war has been the normal state of affairs. In the 64 years since the end of WW II, we have started and fought far more wars and invaded and bombed more countries than any other nation in the world . . . .History will have no choice but to view the U.S.—particularly in its late imperial stages—as a war-fighting state.[52]

Militarization, national arrogance, and the distorted power of the national security establishment, in other words, did not begin or end with George W. Bush. "Bush and those around him have reaffirmed the preexisting fundamentals of U.S. policy, above all the ideology of national security to which past administrations have long subscribed," Andrew Bacevich writes.[53] American exceptionalism, U.S. interventionism, and grossly inflated defense spending have been considered normal by majorities in both parties for many decades. And they have been championed as part of a war culture by a willing media and populace since at least World War II. "The theory that Americans are better than everybody else is endorsed by an overwhelming majority of U.S. voters and approximately 100 percent of all U.S. politicians, although there is less and less to support it," Michael Kinsley writes.[54]

Bacevich says U.S. leaders live by an "American credo" that has "become a de facto prerequisite for high office." The credo "summons the United States—and the United States alone—to lead, save, liberate, and ultimately transform the world." This worldview or credo has guided U.S. policy makers for at least sixty years and has been expressed in the "abiding conviction that the minimum essentials of international peace and order require the United States to maintain a global military presence, to configure its forces for global power projection, and to counter existing or anticipated threats by relying on a policy of global interventionism."[55] The minimum essential is not just a global military presence, but overwhelming military supremacy, which "obliges the United States to maintain military capabilities staggeringly in excess of those required for self-defense."[56]

Militarism continues to dominate our values, mind-set, economy, foreign policies, and lives without regard to political party or president. It is truly bipartisan as evidenced by increased military spending and expanded wars during the Obama administration. Obama embraces the "national security consensus to which every president since 1945 has subscribed," Bacevich writes.[57] Obama's rhetoric is Bush-like when it comes to justifying militarization and war. As the United States institutionalized its ongoing occupation of Iraq and escalated dramatically its war and occupation of Afghanistan, Obama said: "For unlike the great powers of old, we have not sought world domination. Our union was founded in resistance to oppression. We do not seek to occupy other nations." This is "the way we prefer to see ourselves," Bacevich writes. It is the "narrative that we use to justify all that we do in the world." That Obama, "whose background was so different, would embrace that narrative so uncritically" was a clear sign of how little change would come to Washington.[58]

> Paradoxically, the belief that all (or even much) will be well, if only the right person assumes the reins as president and commander in chief serves to underwrite the status quo. Counting on the next president to fix whatever is broken promotes expectations of easy, no cost cures, permitting ordinary citizens to absolve themselves of responsibility for the nation's predicament . . . Rather than seeing the imperial presidency as part of the problem, they persist in the fantasy that a chief executive, given a clear mandate, will "change" the way Washington works and restore the nation to good health.[59]

President Obama was forced to end the occupation of Iraq. He escalated the war in Afghanistan, spread fighting into Pakistan, Yemen, and Libya, and significantly expanded deployment of special operations forces to more than seventy-five countries. Colonel Tim Nye, U.S. special operations command spokesman, says U.S. clandestine warfare is likely to spread soon to 120 nations.[60] President Obama also increased military spending to historic highs, committed $80 billion to upgrade America's nuclear arsenal, and dramatically escalated counterinsurgency warfare, including drone attacks. Philip Alston, UN special rapporteur on extrajudicial executions, warns that drone attacks "may well violate international humanitarian law and international human rights law." The really "problematic bottom line" at present is "that the CIA is running a program that is killing significant numbers of people and there is absolutely no accountability."[61] It is also problematic that drone warfare, like so many other aspects of militarized foreign policies, are counterproductive. Noor Behram, a Pakistani who has photographed the typical aftermath of deadly drone attacks describes the scene:

> There are just pieces of flesh lying around after a strike. You can't find bodies. So the locals pick up the flesh and curse America. They say America is killing us inside our own country, inside our own homes, and only because we are Muslims. The youth in the area surrounding a strike get crazed. Hatred builds up inside those who have seen a drone attack. The Americans think it is working, but the damage they're doing is far greater.[62]

Canadian journalist Eric Margolis notes that "more empires have fallen because of reckless finances than invasion."[63] He estimates that U.S. security spending is about $1 trillion a year.[64] If you factor in interest payments on the nation's debt that are linked to years of excessive "defense" spending the annual trillion dollar figure may be an underestimate.

LIVING BEYOND NEEDS AND MEANS

The United States has been living beyond its *needs* for a very long time. George Kennan, the most important foreign policy planner in the post–World War II period, noted in 1948 that the United States had less than 6 percent of the world's people but nearly half its wealth. "In this situation, we cannot fail to be the object of envy and resentment. Our real task in the coming period is to devise a pattern of relationships which will permit us to maintain this position of disparity." To do so U.S. foreign policy would need to be guided by "straight power concepts." We "should cease to talk about vague and . . . unreal objectives such as human rights, the raising of living standards and democratization."[65]

Fast forward more than sixty years and the United States lives well beyond its *means* as well as its needs. Andrew Bacevich refers to this as a "crisis of profligacy."[66] With about 4.5 percent of the world's people we continue to claim the right to use a quarter of the world's oil (nearly two-thirds imported) and a disproportionate share of many other resources. We have transitioned from being an empire of production to an empire of consumption. A militarized "empire has seemingly become a prerequisite of freedom [to consume]."[67]

U.S. foreign policies intersect with ecology when they defend interests and a global order linked to unsustainable consumption and the relentless pursuit of growth. As Thomas Friedman writes approvingly: "Attention Kmart shoppers: Without America on duty, there will be no America online." "McDonald's can't flourish without McDonnell Douglas, the designer of the U.S. Air Force F-15."[68] In this context U.S. foreign policies are part of a broader war in which the earth itself is targeted or experiences collateral damage. "When we think of wars in our times, our minds turn to Iraq and Afghanistan. But the bigger war is the war against the planet," Indian ecologist Vandana Shiva writes. "This war has its roots in an economy that fails to respect ecological and ethical limits—limits to inequality, limits to injustice, limits to greed and economic concentration."[69] "We have two choices," Donald Rumsfeld said. "Either we change the way we live, or we must change the way they live. We choose the latter."[70] Bacevich writes:

> The collective capacity of our domestic economy to satisfy those appetites has not kept pace with demand. As a result, sustaining our pursuit of life, liberty, and happiness at home requires increasingly that Americans look beyond our borders. Whether the issue at hand is oil, credit, or the availability of cheap consumer goods, we expect the world to accommodate the American way of life.[71]

In this context foreign policy becomes "an expression of domestic dysfunction—an attempt to manage or defer coming to terms with contradictions besetting the American way of life."[72] It's not working. As Bacevich writes, "The exercise of military power will not enable the United States to evade the predicament to which the crisis of profligacy has given rise. To persist in following that path is to invite inevitable overextension, bankruptcy, and ruin."[73] We desperately need humility and a reality check. The United States has no special calling to justify militarization, interventionism, and war. It has no economic capacity to continue on the dead-end road of militarization. It has no effective military means or strategies to effectively address serious domestic and global problems. It has no security need that can be met with reckless militarization. The national security establishment, far from defending the nation, has become the principle obstacle to a decent social order and to authentic security.

RECOGNIZING LIMITS

Emmanuel Todd saw the economic foundations of empire crumbling and the limitations of U.S. military power. A few U.S. politicians get it. "Estimates for the total direct and indirect costs of the wars in Afghanistan and Iraq by their end range from $5 trillion to $7 trillion with more than 5,700 Americans having given their lives in these conflicts," Congresswoman Barbara Lee writes. It is "clear we cannot accept a policy of open-ended war without accepting a less prosperous, less secure country for ourselves and future generations."[74] "The Constitution does not give us the authority to be the policeman of the world," Ron Paul says. "We spend a trillion dollars a year maintaining an empire, but we're broke."[75] When it comes to addressing American exceptionalism or militarized foreign policies generally, most U.S. leaders are spineless or conveniently clueless. As retired Lieutenant Colonel William J. Astore writes:

> It's time to stop deferring to our generals, and even to their commander and chief. . . . Yet when it comes to tough questioning of the president's generals. . . . Senators and representatives are

invariably too busy falling all over themselves praising our troops and their commanders, too worried that "tough" questioning will appear unpatriotic to the folks back home, or too connected to military contractors in their districts, or some combination of the three.[76]

Addressing the distorted power of a national security establishment on steroids and the wide gulf separating material aspirations from the actual potential of both the economy and ecology will open up possibilities for soft landings. Until we do so, however, we can expect living standards to erode further and militarization and war to dominate our lives no matter which political party is in the majority or who occupies the White House. Stephen L. Carter in a *Newsweek* article, "Man of War," wrote that "Obama might have run in 2008 as the peace candidate, but next time around he will be running as a war president." "Strip away the soaring rhetoric," he said, and you will see that Obama differs "as a commander in chief from his swaggering predecessor . . . a lot less than you might think."[77]

Carter said this is true because all presidents discover that their primary duty is to keep the nation safe. An alternative explanation is far more compelling, but can't be said in polite company: in a war culture such as ours excessive influence resides in the military industrial complex and all presidents have chosen to defer to the national security establishment. "Pretending the role of Decider, a president all too often becomes little more than the medium through which power is exercised," Bacevich writes. "Especially on matters related to national security, others manufacture or manipulate situations to which presidents then react."[78]

A scene from Bob Woodward's book *Obama's War* illustrates perfectly this point. Obama has asked his national security team for options on Afghanistan. They present him with multiple scenarios but only one option: escalation. Obama seems reluctant to embrace their plans. Army Colonel John Tien reminds him who's in charge:

Mr. President, I don't see how you can defy your military chain here. We kind of are where we are. Because if you tell General McChrystal, "I got your assessment, got your resource constructs, but I've chosen to do something else," you're going to probably have to replace him. You can't tell him, "Just do it my way, thanks for your hard work." And then where does that stop.

Woodward continues:

The colonel did not have to elaborate. His implication was that not only McChrystal but the entire military high command might go in an unprecedented toppling—Gates; Adm. Mike Mullen, the chairman of the Joint Chiefs of Staff; and Gen. David H. Petraeus, then head of the U.S. Central Command. Perhaps no president could weather that, especially a 48-year-old with four years in the U.S. Senate and 10 months as commander in chief.[79]

This shouldn't surprise us. As Bacevich writes, "the range of acceptable opinion in a typical faculty lounge is orders of magnitude greater than that which prevails in precincts where U.S. national security policy gets discussed and formulated."[80] He also reminds us that the beneficiaries of what he calls "Washington rules" and membership in the formal and informal echelons of the national security state apparatus today are far more expansive than anything President Eisenhower could have imagined when he warned the nation about the rising power of the military industrial complex. Benefits can't simply be measured "in cold cash or political influence," Bacevich writes. They are "psychic as well as substantive. For many, the payoff includes the added, if largely illusory, attraction of occupying a seat within or near what is imagined to be the very cockpit of contemporary history. Before power corrupts it attracts and then seduces." He asks and answers a question: Who benefits from the perpetuation of the Washington rules?

Washington itself benefits. The Washington rules deliver profit, power, and privilege to a long list of beneficiaries: elected and appointed officials, corporate executives and corporate lobbyists, admirals and generals, functionaries staffing the national security apparatus, media personalities, and policy intellectuals from universities and research organizations. Each year the Pentagon expends hundreds of billions of dollars to raise and support U.S. military forces. This money lubricates American politics, filling campaign coffers and providing a source of largesse—jobs and contracts—for distribution to constituents. It provides lucrative "second careers" for retired U.S. military officers hired by weapons manufacturers or by consulting firms appropriately known as "Beltway Bandits." It funds the activities of think tanks that relentlessly advocate for policies guaranteed to fend off challenges to established conventions. "Military industrial complex" no longer suffices to describe the congeries of interests profiting from and committed to preserving the national security status quo.[81]

CONCLUSION

When I spoke at a vigil sponsored by Veterans for Peace at Occupy Minneapolis, I noted that both truth and soldiers are casualties of war. The three most dangerous words a soldier in America can hear, I said, are "support our troops" because what these words generally mean is that we are to stifle dissent while supporting unjust wars, lying presidents, and war profiteers. Uncritical patriotism wrapped up in nationalism is not the friend of soldiers. It is a scoundrel that kills. It is outrageous that we see so many superficial signs of veneration of troops even as soldiers themselves are chewed up, spit out, and abandoned to joblessness and despair. Soldiers and veterans are praised at sporting events as flags cover fields and fighter jets fly overhead, but they are rarely valued, cared for, or listened to.

Unfortunately, "thank you for your service" is too often a source of cheap grace for those who utter the words but can't be bothered to examine the deadly consequences of U.S. foreign policies, the causes of war, or the relationship between war and the military industrial complex. As a result, many soldiers die, not for their country, but because their countrymen and women are swept up in the vulgarities of uncritical patriotism and nationalism. We thank soldiers for their service by working to end senseless wars, by holding leaders accountable for lies, by meeting their physical and emotional needs, and by building a culture of peace.

Militarism is destroying our country and foreclosing on a hopeful future. When a president is faced with members of the national security team manipulating the nation into unnecessary wars, he or she should send them all packing and tell the nation why. Saying good riddance to empire won't be easy but it will offer many benefits. It requires us to challenge the dominant narrative in which citizens are economic consumers and political spectators, war leads to peace, prosperity depends on resources that can be accessed only through power projection, aggressive militarization is national defense, soldiers are being supported when we send them to fight unjust wars, and the military industrial complex is under civilian rule and committed to the nation's security. Fortunately, in the case of militarization and arrogant foreign policies soft landings are possible if we reject American exceptionalism and embrace meaningful alternatives laid out in the next chapter.

Chapter 5

Good Riddance to Empire, Part 2: Possibilities

America doesn't need a bigger army. It needs a smaller—that is, more modest—foreign policy.
—ANDREW BACEVICH[1]

The real question is not whether U.S. hegemony is waning but whether the United States can devise a way to descend gracefully, with minimum damage to the world, and itself.
—IMMANUEL WALLERSTEIN[2]

Permanent war has become the de facto policy of the United States—even as it has become apparent that war does not provide a plausible antidote to the problems facing the United States.
—ANDREW BACEVICH[3]

INTRODUCTION

Saying good riddance to empire will allow us to build a decent future. We are much more likely to do so when we recognize: that militarism isn't defense of the country; American exceptionalism isn't warranted; defending interests doesn't keep us safe; pursuit of global domination undermines economic and social well-being; wars for oil harm us, the environment, and others; and the national security establishment is more interested in power and profits than defense; and there are alternative pathways to authentic security. This chapter describes some of the quality of life benefits of rejecting empire and alternative approaches to foreign policy that would make soft landings possible and our nation and world safer.

UNHEEDED WARNINGS

Martin Luther King and President Dwight Eisenhower differed in background, experience, and vocation but they both decried the high social costs of militarization and war. In one of the greatest speeches ever given by an American, King described how the hopes of the poor were shattered and broken because "of a society gone mad on war." He warned "that America would never invest the necessary funds" to end poverty "so long as adventures like Vietnam continued to draw men and skills and money like some demonic destructive suction tube." King noted that in Vietnam we once again had fallen "victim to the deadly Western arrogance that has poisoned the international atmosphere for so long," that Americans could only be seen "as strange liberators," and that our nation had become "the greatest purveyor of violence in the world." He called for "a radical revolution in values" and noted that a "nation that continues year after year to spend more money on military defense than on programs of social uplift is approaching spiritual death." He warned that "Vietnam is but a symptom of a far deeper malady within the American spirit, and if we ignore this sobering reality we will find ourselves" organizing against other wars "for the next generation."[4]

Some people dismiss King's words as the musings of a radical civil rights leader, but years earlier President Eisenhower voiced similar concerns. "Every gun that is made, every warship launched, every rocket fired signifies, in the final sense, a theft from those who hunger and are not fed, those who are cold and are not clothed. The world in arms is not spending money alone," Eisenhower said in a 1953 speech. "It is spending the sweat of its laborers, the genius of its scientists, the hopes of its children. . . . This is not a way of life at all, in any true sense. Under the cloud of threatening war, it is humanity hanging from a cross of iron."[5]

Eisenhower believed militarism and those who benefited from it could threaten democracy and undermine both human and actual defense needs. In his 1961 farewell address to the country, he warned that the "military industrial complex" could become a serious threat to the nation. The "conjunction of an immense military establishment and a large arms industry is new in the American experience." Its influence—"economic, political, even spiritual—is felt in every city, every Statehouse, every office of the Federal government. . . . " "In the councils of government we must guard against the acquisition of unwarranted influence, whether sought or unsought, by the military industrial complex. The potential for the disastrous rise of misplaced power exists and will persist."[6]

THE ELEPHANT IN THE ROOM

Eisenhower's and King's words are among the most important, unheeded warnings in American history. Authentic hope requires that we take them seriously. The result of ignoring their counsel is that the national security establishment has morphed into a far graver threat. Militarism and misplaced power are bringing our country to ruin. Although saying good riddance to empire will alienate powerful groups who benefit from militarization and war, it is the key to transformation. It offers policy makers and citizens many options to improve quality of life. Rejecting the dead-end road of empire would not only free up resources for other things but also enhance our nation's security. The humbling and potentially liberating truth that can open up possibilities for soft landings is this: *The United States has no moral authority or unique calling, no economic capacity, no military means, and no security need to embrace permanent war, invade and occupy other nations, or continue wasteful military spending.*

There is more good news. There are solutions, but not military solutions, to most of the problems we face. Militarism intensifies problems and prevents meaningful solutions. A bloated military establishment fed with comforting myths of American exceptionalism threatens our security. Demilitarizing our priorities will make it possible to address climate change, build a sustainable economy, revitalize politics, meet the health and education needs of our people, reduce our dependency on foreign oil, build a renewable energy system, promote values of simplicity, compassion, and generosity, create effective international institutions to respond to pressing global needs, preserve the integrity of our land and water resources, enhance security, and diminish terror.

Hardly a day goes by in which I don't lament the obvious signs of decline and our collective failure to connect the dots between unmet needs and wasted dollars on militarization and war. Schools with large and growing class sizes beg parents for toilet paper and school supplies. Bridges collapse or stand in need of urgent repair. Soldiers return from America's wars and take their own lives in record numbers. Hunger and homelessness increase as food shelves struggle to keep up with demand. Cities and states cut essential services. Unemployment becomes a permanent fact of life. Firefighters, police, and teachers lose their jobs. Critical infrastructure, and green technologies receive minimal investments. Public libraries close or restrict hours. Urban and national rail systems aren't built. Bizarre weather patterns consistent with climate change proliferate while effective responses languish. One in five U.S. children lives in poverty. Millions of Americans lack affordable health care.

These and other unmet needs seem to run on a track that is parallel to another marked by hyper-patriotism and funding for unnecessary wars. Obscene levels of military spending beyond any reasonable measure of legitimate defense are the elephant in the room of which few are willing to speak. The United States with about 4.5 percent of the world's people accounts for nearly half of global military spending and nearly 70 percent of global weapons sales.[7] Approximately 58 cents of every dollar in the federal discretionary budget is devoted to militarism and war.[8] Militarism and social decay do not travel on parallel tracks. They intersect at thousands of points with unmet needs, the visible signs of imperial decline.

Nicholas Kristof says America has chosen militarism over health care. Forty five thousand Americans die each year because of our dysfunctional health care system and as many "people die every three weeks from lack of health insurance as were killed in the 9/11 attacks." He asks if we are better off "blowing up things in Helmand Province or building up things in America?" Which "is the greater danger to our homeland security, the Taliban or our dysfunctional insurance system?"[9] Congresswoman Barbara Lee writes similarly: "Every additional dollar invested in war is a dollar we take away from much-needed investments in health care, education, infrastructure and clean energy that will preserve and create high-quality jobs, as well as ensure America's future competitiveness."[10]

Imagine what we can accomplish if we remove the elephant from the room, say good riddance to empire, and stop squandering wealth and talents on militarization and counterproductive wars. Schools will reduce class sizes and have adequate supplies. Bridges will be repaired. The nation will significantly reduce the size of the military. Soldiers will be involved in national defense, not power projection. Food shelves will be rarely needed. Homelessness will be unusual and temporary. Cities and states will have sufficient resources to provide essential services. More firefighters, police, and teachers will be hired as the nation invests in the authentic security needs of communities and the nation. Critical investments will be made in infrastructure and green technologies. Public libraries will expand hours and programming. Urban and national rail systems will be built. The country will address climate change. The child poverty rate will plummet. All Americans will have access to quality, affordable health care.

This is a fantasy only because we choose to continue on the dead-end road of militarization, which constricts possibilities and stifles hope. It is a realistic possibility once we demilitarize our priorities and refocus governing on serving the common good and refocus our lives on purposeful living. Saying good riddance to empire will allow us to enhance our nation's security, meet essential needs, and achieve soft landings.

MINNESOTA NICE

Minnesotans have a reputation for being nice, but the political climate in my state is ugly. Year after year elected officials do mean-spirited things to balance the state's budget as required by law. Balanced budgets are generally achieved through some combination of cuts in social spending and services, under-investment in essential infrastructure, and financial gimmickry that shifts costs onto local communities, the poor, and future budgets. The causes of fiscal difficulties are many, including the high costs of a dysfunctional health care system. Among the main causes, however, are changes in the tax code that slash income tax rates which reduce government revenues year after year. Mirroring federal policies these tax cuts are highly skewed in favor of the wealthiest citizens. The economic meltdown that began in 2007 accelerated these trends as rising levels of unemployment further reduced tax revenues. A grave situation would have been worse without a temporary influx of federal stimulus funds.

Budget difficulties are consequences of a perverse ideology promoting so-called limited government, which led to a spiral of tax cuts followed by budget cuts. A "no new taxes" Republican governor with national political ambitions blocked all efforts to raise revenues and slashed funding for essential programs, including support payments to Minnesota cities. This led to a domino effect in which budget problems were shifted onto local governments, which were then forced to increase property taxes, and cut budgets, staff, and services.

Minnesota politicians faced another budget shortfall of approximately $5 billion for the two-year period of 2011–12. Many of their proposed solutions, despite protests from a recently elected governor (Democrat Mark Dayton), relied heavily on a new cycle of budget cuts that would further erode living standards. Similar dynamics were at play in many other states, and deficit hawks also dominated the debate in Washington with efforts to gut social security well under way. The actions of elected officials at all levels, including both Democrats and Republicans, further eroded the quality of life for many Americans, starting with the most vulnerable. "It has become fashionable among politicians to preach the virtues of pain and suffering," writes economist Joseph Stiglitz, "no doubt because those bearing the brunt are those with little voice—the poor and future generations."[11]

The pain is spreading to a much wider swath of Americans as the consequences of inequality become more visible and the economic crisis deepens. Well-organized elites, whose greed and malfeasance generally caused or aggravated the economic crisis, have sufficient influence over public policies to block necessary reforms or to orchestrate "solutions" that expand their privileges while dumping austerity onto others. This creates widespread anxiety, anger, and poorly targeted resentments that fuel regressive politics. A downward spiral (always evident during a period of imperial decline) accelerates as "fiscal constraints" require more pain for average citizens, while the rich expand their share of national wealth and income, and the Pentagon fills in what amounts to a blank check.

The result of this unfortunate and ongoing spiral is that militarization walks hand in hand on a dead-end road with a politics of scarcity that dominates national and local politics. Elected officials and pundits of all stripes chime in with proposals that range from somewhat reasonable to the theater of the absurd. Situated among the latter are politicians who scream bloody murder about deficits undermining the country's future while happily feeding the insatiable appetite of the Pentagon and extending tax breaks to corporations and the super-rich, including the richest 1 percent, who already receive nearly a quarter of the nation's income.[12] As Stiglitz writes:

> The attempt to restrain the growth of debt does serve to concentrate the mind: It forces countries to focus on priorities and assess

values . . . Technically, reducing a deficit is a straightforward matter: One must either cut expenditures or raise taxes. It is already
clear, however, that the deficit-reduction agenda, at least in the
United States, goes further: It is an attempt to weaken social pro-
tections, reduce the progressivity of the tax system, and shrink
the role and size of government—*all while leaving established
interests, like the military-industrial complex, as little-affected as
possible.*[13]

As we saw in chapters 2 and 3, there are many practical policies
and pathways to improve quality of life in fiscally and environmentally responsible ways as we move to a more equitable, sustainable, less
militarized society. To fully do so, however, we need to move from a
war culture that inevitably fuels a politics of scarcity to a peace culture
that promotes a progressive politics of possibility, generosity, and suf-
ficiency. This requires us to connect the dots that link declining empire,
national insecurity, deepening fiscal crises, high unemployment, and
reduced living standards to counterproductive wars and absurd levels of
military spending.

With this background let me return to the example of the elephant in the
room and Minnesota politicians facing a two-year budget shortfall of $5
billion. Eager Republicans and reluctant Democrats temporarily resolved
the "budget crisis" by further shredding the social fabric of the state. No
one from either political party mentioned the elephant until a citizen-based
initiative pointed out that Minnesota taxpayers during this same two-year
period would pay approximately $26 billion for their share of the base U.S.
defense budget.[14] This $26 billion doesn't include the cost of the ongo-
ing wars in Iraq or Afghanistan. These wars had cost Minnesota taxpayers
nearly $27 billion as of the end of December 2010 and would cost them an
additional $8.4 billion during the two-year budget period in question, $3.4
billion more than the state's entire budget shortfall.[15]

Much was made of California's budget deficit of $19.1 billion for
2011, which led to dramatic cuts in essential services. California's

proposed share of the 2011 defense budget was $93.4 billion! Califor-
nia's contribution to the wars in Iraq and Afghanistan as of the end of
January 2011 was nearly $145 billion, and in 2011 California taxpay-
ers were set to pay $21.8 billion for the wars in Iraq and Afghanistan,
$2.7 billion more than the state's entire budget deficit.[16] The National
Priorities Project reports that in 2011 forty-six states faced cumulative
budget shortfalls of $130 billion while the Obama administration pro-
posed another $170 billion to pay for wars in Iraq and Afghanistan.[17] Or
consider this report from CNN:

> The mayor of crime-ridden Camden, New Jersey, has announced
> layoffs of nearly half of the city's police force and close to a third
> of its fire department. One hundred sixty-eight police officers and
> sixty-seven firefighters were laid off Tuesday, as officials struggle
> to close a $26.5 million budget gap through a series of belt-tight-
> ening measures, Mayor Dana Redd told reporters. The layoffs take
> effect immediately.[18]

Citizens of Camden County, New Jersey, had paid nearly $2.75 billion
for their share of the Iraq and Afghanistan Wars, and their share of the
defense budget for 2011 was $1.8 billion. Citizens of the state would pay
$33.7 billion to the Defense Department in 2011.[19]

I know of course that the federal budget is a separate entity from state,
county, and city budgets. My point is that in a war culture militarized
priorities at the national level negatively impact budgets and quality of
life at all levels of government and society. It is a fiction to claim that distorted, militarized priorities at the federal government level aren't connected to local, county, and state budget woes. In an article entitled "Do
You Feel Safer Yet?" Tom Engelhardt writes:

> In the U.S., policemen and firemen are being laid off, and the police
> and fire departments cut back or, in a few small places, eliminated.
> In Afghanistan, the U.S., having already invested $20 billion in
> building up the Afghan police and military, is now planning to

spend $11.6 billion more this year alone, $12.8 billion in 2012, and more than $6 billion a year thereafter. According to Washington's latest scheme, the Afghan security forces will be increased to 378,000 men in a poverty-stricken land, which means committing U.S. tax dollars to the project into the distant future. Do you feel safer?[20]

OPPORTUNITIES

It is tempting to feel hopeless in the presence of powerful forces that benefit from militarization and war or to blame others for our predicament, but as citizens we must see ourselves as responsible actors. The "onus of responsibility falls squarely on us," Bacevich writes. History "will not judge kindly a people who find nothing amiss in the prospect of endless war. . . . Nor will it view with favor an electorate that delivers political power into the hands of leaders unable to envision any alternative to perpetual war." "Rather than insisting that the world accommodate to the United States," he writes, "Americans need to reassert control over their destiny, ending their condition of dependency and abandoning their imperial ambitions."[21]

Nor should we let the magnitude of the current crisis blind us to possibilities in the present moment. We are in a period in which solutions are unlikely to emerge from or be allowed by present political leaders or the economic or national security interests to which they are beholden. Nonetheless, these troubling times are ripe for building a social movement capable of bringing about necessary changes. In a Gallup poll from September 2010 more than 60 percent of respondents named the economy in general or jobs and unemployment as "the most important problem facing this country today." Only 3 percent cited war or fear of war.[22] An ABC/*Washington Post* poll in December showed 60 percent of Americans saying the war in Afghanistan "was not worth fighting."[23] A January 2011 *New York Times*/CBS poll showed "a majority by a large margin said cut the Pentagon" rather than Social Security or Medicare.[24] And yet, as Robert Koehler says, "the machinery of empire grinds on."[25]

The pressing need is to connect the dots between unnecessary wars and economic insecurities. A militarized empire will never have a healthy economy. Its priorities fuel economic and social decline. It doesn't keep us safe. It has no future. Once we recognize this, and it is increasingly difficult to ignore, we can joyfully say good riddance. It's the end of the world as we know it but soft landings are possible. Rejecting militarized empire opens up tremendous possibilities for meaningful change. I never buy lottery tickets, but I do occasionally fantasize about all the good I could do if I won and gave the money to groups doing important work. Think of saying good riddance to empire as equivalent to the nation winning the lottery, everyday, forever. Think of what we could do. Think of what needs to be done.

PRACTICAL POLICIES

We have the power to choose to be a country guided by better values and different priorities. The remainder of the chapter describes practical policies and realistic pathways to authentic security based on the analysis in this and the previous chapter.

Embrace Humility. Reject American Exceptionalism

Our foreign policies and approach to global issues and affairs should be guided by humility, not arrogance. The world doesn't want or need the United States to be a global cop, dominate the world, or act alone. We have no right, capacity, or security need to do so. Humility, economic necessity, and authentic security needs require us to reject arrogant claims of American exceptionalism, end foreign occupations, dismantle much of our network of global bases, oppose military interventionism, avoid double standards, and set out to build a truly sustainable society.

Embrace Global Partnerships. Reject Unilateralism

Global partnerships are the proper foundation of national security, not unilateralism. The single most important security decision a nation makes is whether to seek security in the context of international rules, laws, and agreements or by claiming the right to act alone. The United States claims rights for itself not granted to any other nation. U.S. ambition, including efforts to maintain privileges and expand influence through aggressive militarism, threatens U.S. and international peace and security. That is why Gwynne Dyer, a well-respected Canadian analyst and friend of the United States, wrote shortly after the U.S. invasion of Iraq: "The United States needs to lose the war in Iraq as soon as possible. Even more urgently, the whole world needs the United States to lose the war in Iraq. . . . What is at stake is the way we run the world for the next generation or more, and really bad things will happen if we get it wrong."[26] Although there is no such thing as absolute security, both our nation and the world will be safer when the United States rejects empire. The alternative to militarized empire and unilateralism isn't disengagement or isolationism. It is a more modest international role rooted in global partnerships and international law.

I try to imagine the response of leaders of other nations, especially China, when they read a document like "Rebuilding America's Defenses" (RAD) or hear U.S. leaders claim a moral right and practical intention to dominate the world. Or consider the reverse. If China or Russia or Iran made such claims our leaders would go ballistic, both literally and figuratively. Influential journalist Robert Kaplan wrote approvingly that by the turn of the century the Pentagon had "appropriated the entire earth, and was ready to flood the most obscure areas of it with troops at a moment's notice." The whole earth had become "battle space for the American military."[27]

Others surely know that frequent verbal provocations laced with imperial ambition are not just fantasies. The United States spends almost as much on militarism and war as the rest of the world combined.

It stands in the way of an international consensus to keep space for peaceful purposes. It announces strategies that target nations for nuclear attack. It exempts its leaders and soldiers from jurisdiction of the International Criminal Court. It ignores the Geneva Conventions and redefines and engages in torture with no accountability. It invades and occupies other nations with impunity. It routinely intervenes in the affairs of other nations seeking oil and influence. It dots the globe with more than 750 foreign military bases and stations soldiers in 175 countries. It carries out drone attacks and targeted assassinations in dozens of countries in violation of international laws. It declares global ambitions, divides the world into six areas, and organizes its military to project power accordingly.[28] As Tom Engelhardt notes, "There is no imaginable space on or off the planet that is not an 'area of responsibility' for the U.S. military."[29]

The United States for decades has engaged in an arms race with itself. This has done grave harm to our economy, and it will inevitably trigger a backlash. The United States can ill afford an arms race with China or any other nation. And both our country and the world have many pressing needs that will only be met if U.S. and world military spending is redirected to meet them. Within the logic of U.S. war culture, however, any battlefield setback is reason for further military escalation, and any increase in another nation's military capacity is viewed as a provocation and challenge to U.S. power and interests. There is an easy way to break this spiral. Refuse double standards and join the community of nations.

It is long past time for the United States to scale back arrogant ambitions and global military presence. Choosing a more modest global role within the framework of international laws and agreements offers the only real prospect for peace, security, and soft landings. There are no military solutions to the problems we face and no non-military solutions without acknowledging this fact. It is time to say good riddance to empire and join the community of nations as a good global partner.

Focus on Legitimate Defense

We need a Department of Defense that focuses on legitimate defense. At present we have a War Department and national security state apparatus committed to power projection and to scandalous profits for their members and allies. The good news is that the United States could defend its borders and meet any legitimate security need for a fraction of current military costs. Mark Thompson in a 2011 article in *Time* ("How to Save a Trillion Dollars") describes how easy it would be to make cuts in a bloated military establishment that is producing many weapons systems the country doesn't need.[30] His modest proposals based on minimal reductions over a ten-year period barely scratch the surface of what is possible if we reject empire and focus on authentic security. As Thompson notes, for "too long, an uninterested and distracted citizenry has been content to leave the messy business of national defense to those with bottom-line reasons for force-feeding it like a foie gras goose."[31] Reductions in the range of 70 to 80 percent are in order. The Stockholm International Peace Research Institute 2010 report shows the United States accounted for 46.5 percent of global military spending. China was second with 6.6 percent. That means the United States could have reduced military spending by 70 percent and still been the world's military spending leader.[32]

The reason cuts of this magnitude are possible is simple. Present foreign policies and military spending levels are completely disconnected from any reasonable assessment of threat or security need. They are dictated by ambition, including the desire to control the world's shrinking energy resources, and by the needs of a national security state establishment. This insight explains why the United States continues its disastrous policies in Iraq and Afghanistan. The pretense of winning has been replaced with a commitment to permanent occupation and war. "I don't think you win this war," General Petraeus says casually. "I think you keep fighting. . . . This is the kind of fight we're in for the rest of our lives and probably our kids' lives." Bacevich asks the logical question:

"Why fight a war that even the general in charge says can't be won? It is a question never asked but the answer is rather easy. War is a source of enormous wealth and power."[33]

If our leaders acknowledged the breadth and depth of the multiple catastrophes spewing from these wars it would undermine the American credo that has dominated U.S. foreign policy and been the source of power and profits for sixty years. America claims a unique right to lead the world. And to do so and to meet its own security needs it says it must maintain military supremacy, configure its forces to project global power, and intervene constantly in the affairs of other nations. "If we have to use force," Madeline Albright asserted, "it is because we are America! We are the indispensable nation!"[34] It should now be clear that "campaigns in Afghanistan and Iraq intended to showcase an unprecedented mastery of war;" Bacevich writes, "demonstrated the folly of imagining that war could be mastered."[35] A major impetus for continuing these wars is to prevent a complete collapse that would delegitimize the credo itself. This would make clear that militarism is not defense. It would expose the national security state apparatus as the gravest threat to our security and the leading cause of economic, social, and spiritual decline. And it would hasten the movement to say good riddance to empire and to choose alternative pathways.

End America's Oil Addiction

Ending America's oil addiction would have many positive outcomes, including the fact it would allow for dramatic reductions in military spending and profound changes in U.S. foreign policies. The United States, with about 4.5 percent of the world's people and 3 percent of global oil reserves, uses approximately 25 percent of the world's oil. In 2009, it borrowed and spent nearly $265 billion to pay its oil import bill, more than half a million dollars a minute.[36] This is only a fraction of the actual cost of imported oil. Oil addiction and energy concerns drive most U.S. foreign policies. Reducing oil dependency and use would allow the

United States each year to save hundreds of billions of dollars in war and power projection costs. Even Alan Greenspan, Republican and former head of the Federal Reserve, stated in his memoirs: "I am saddened that it is politically inconvenient to acknowledge what everyone knows: the Iraq war is largely about oil."[37] So too is the war in Afghanistan.

Americans need to investigate more carefully why the United States is involved in the longest war in its history in a country UNICEF says "is the worst place in the world to be born, having the highest infant mortality rate in the world with 257 deaths per 1,000 live births."[38] Let's first note that it's not primarily about al Qaeda, or the Taliban, or keeping us safe. Admiral James Jones, President Obama's first national security advisor, said: "I don't foresee the return of the Taliban. Afghanistan is not in imminent danger of falling. . . .The al-Qaeda presence is very diminished. The maximum estimate is less than 100 operating in the country, no bases, no ability to launch attacks on either us or our allies."[39] Anand Gopal, *Wall Street Journal* correspondent in Afghanistan, says it is also important to realize that "Al Qaeda and the Taliban are groups with distinct ideologies and goals." The central goal of the Taliban is "to kick out the Americans."[40] A *Boston Globe* article reports: "Nearly all of the insurgents battling US and NATO troops in Afghanistan are not religiously motivated Taliban and Al Qaeda warriors, but a new generation of tribal fighters vying for control of territory, mineral wealth, and smuggling routes, according to summaries of new US intelligence reports." U.S. intelligence indicates that 90 percent of Taliban fighters in Afghanistan are "a tribal, localized insurgency." They "see themselves as opposing the US because it is an occupying power." They have "no goals" beyond Afghanistan's borders."[41]

So why is the United States waging war in Afghanistan? The U.S. agenda, Robert Koehler writes, "includes regional dominance, the flow of oil (the pipeline), and, as with every war, the stoking of the military economy."[42] John Foster, with the Canadian Centre for Policy Alternatives, has written a detailed analysis of U.S. goals and motives that center on energy and pipeline politics: "Afghanistan," he writes, "has a key role in the quest for access to the immense energy resources of Central Asia."[43] Afghanistan has been a frequent battleground between nations and empires vying for dominance of the region. In efforts to conquer Afghanistan, foreign powers have expended great sums in blood and treasure. Today, the Great Game is a quest for control of energy export routes. Afghanistan is an energy bridge to bring natural gas from Turkmenistan to Pakistan and India.[44]

The stakes in the Great Game are who gets to control pipeline routes to transport the region's vast energy resources. The United States wants control, and it wants to keep China, Russia, and Iran out. Richard Boucher, U.S. assistant secretary of state for South and Central Asian Affairs said: "One of our goals is to stabilize Afghanistan, so it can become a conduit and a hub between South and Central Asia so that energy can flow to the south."[45] The problem is the pipeline route preferred by the United States runs through conflict zones in Afghanistan where the United States and the Afghan government are despised by many.

U.S. leaders have every intention of having an enduring presence in Iraq and Afghanistan. Robert Naiman, director of Just Foreign Policy, writes in the context of the ongoing occupation of Iraq, that U.S. leaders "see it as an immutable fact of life on Earth that the U.S. must try to control the governments of the broader Middle East, even if the attempt to do so produces terrible violence." This problem is "more relevant today, because we are still pursuing a policy in Afghanistan that is based on the same premise: the United States government can and must determine who will participate in power in Afghanistan."[46]

Expansion of U.S. military bases may be the best indicator of U.S. intentions: "Three $100 million air base expansions in southern and northern Afghanistan illustrate Pentagon plans to continue building multimillion-dollar facilities in that country to support increased U.S. military operations well into the future," Walter Pincus writes.[47] Michael Klare examined the Obama administration's Quadrennial Defense

Review and concluded that it lays out U.S. plans to conduct aggressive counterinsurgency operations worldwide "for decades to come." What "should be cause for alarm is that despite the worrisome picture of Afghanistan, the Pentagon is determined to export this model to other areas, many for the first time, including Africa."[48]

Another important way in which energy and oil concerns intersect with foreign policy is that a military committed to supremacy and global power projection runs on oil. "The U.S. military is the world's single biggest consumer of fossil fuels, and the single entity most responsible for destabilizing the Earth's climate," Joseph Nevins writes. The Pentagon "devours about 330,000 barrels of oil per day, more than the vast majority of the world's countries. If the U.S. military were a nation-state, it would be ranked number 37 in terms of consumption."[49]

Ironically, in recent years the Pentagon, which together with the rest of the United States is a leading consumer of oil and thus a major contributor to climate change, has consistently sounded the alarm that climate changes will likely dramatically increase social instability and threaten U.S. security interests. Unfortunately, the Pentagon strongly resists redirecting military spending to efforts to prevent climate change or help nations to adapt. They are demanding more resources for counterinsurgency and special operations forces. Christian Parenti writes that the "Pentagon is planning for a world remade by climate change. You could even say the Pentagon is planning for Armageddon." The implications are frightening:

> The Pentagon and its European allies are actively planning a militarized adaptation, which emphasizes the long-term, open-ended containment of failed or failing states—counterinsurgency forever. This sort of "climate fascism," a politics based on exclusion, segregation, and repression, is horrific and bound to fail. The struggling states of the Global South cannot collapse without taking wealthy economies down with them. If climate change is allowed to destroy whole economies and nations, no amount of walls, guns,

barbed wire, armed aerial drones, or permanently deployed merce-
naries will be able to save one half of the planet from the other."[50]

Breaking our oil dependency, helping the world transition from
carbon-based fuels to renewable energy, and freeing up resources to
mitigate the consequences of global warming could also encourage a
cooperative relationship with China and other energy-hungry nations.
Militarizing efforts to address the consequences of climate change or
fruitlessly trying to control and access shrinking oil supplies through
aggressive militarization will mean needless and dangerous conflict.
This is no small matter because how the United States and China choose
to deal with oil, energy, military, and climate will likely determine the
future of the world. And as Michael Klare writes: "China's efforts to
bolster its ties with its foreign-oil providers have produced geopolitical
friction with the United States. There is a risk of far more serious Sino-
American conflict as we enter the tough oil era and the world supply of
easily accessible petroleum rapidly shrinks."[51]

Klare writes that the leading global energy users are involved in
"the energy equivalent of an arms race to secure control over whatever
remaining deposits of oil and natural gas are up for sale on the planet,
along with reserves of other materials. This resource race," he writes, "is
already one of the most conspicuous features of the contemporary political landscape and, in our lifetimes, may become *the* most conspicuous
one—a voracious, zero-sum contest that, if allowed to continue along
present paths, can only lead to conflict among the major powers."[52] The
good news is that it "is possible to imagine a future in which China
and the United States cooperate in pursuing oil alternatives that would
obviate the need to funnel massive sums into naval and military arms
races."[53]

Change Ourselves First

The authentic security of the United States will be enhanced greatly
if we reject militarized empire and change our policies and behaviors.

Militarism is not defense. It makes us less secure. For example, militarism is a poor way to deal with terrorism or so-called rogue states. Alternative ways of doing so involve addressing the causes of terror and the legitimate concerns of such states. Michael Mann in his book *Incoherent Empire* writes that the world isn't nearly as dangerous as many Americans are led to fear and it would be even less dangerous if it weren't for American militarism:

> It should not be dangerous at all for Americans—so prosperous, so comfortable and so well-protected in the sea-girded continent we dominate. Dangers loom *because* of American militarism—seeking to drive into the ground the few failing communist remnants in the world, seeking extra-territorial control over oil supplies, stationing American troops where they have no business, invading foreign countries uninvited and supporting state terrorists. No significant danger would occur if the US stopped doing all these things. Quite the contrary.[54]

U.S. military dominance makes terrorism a logical form of resistance for groups who have grievances with the United States. In 1998, Presidential Decision Directive 62 stated: "America's unrivaled military superiority means that potential enemies (whether nations or terrorist groups) that choose to attack us will be more likely to resort to terror instead of conventional military assault."[55] A similar conclusion was reached by the Defense Science Board in 1997: "Historical data show a strong correlation between U.S. involvement in international situations and an increase in terrorist attacks against the United States. In addition, the military asymmetry that denies nation states the ability to engage in overt attacks against the United States drives the use of transnational actors."[56]

President Bush told the nation on September 11, 2001, that "America was targeted for attack because we're the brightest beacon for freedom and opportunity in the world."[57] This explanation is a classic example of how the myth of American exceptionalism places platitudes above security. "The preferred American story," John Esposito writes, is that the terrorists "own history, backwardness, poverty and cultural resentment causes terrorism—so that we do not even have to listen to what they say are their actual grievances."[58] Our policies, not our ideals, make us targets of international terrorism. An unclassified study published by the Pentagon-appointed Defense Science Board on September 23, 2004, stated: *"Muslims do not 'hate our freedom,' but rather our policies. The overwhelming majority voice their objections to what they see as one-sided support in favor of Israel and against Palestinian rights, and the longstanding, even, increasing support for what Muslims collectively see as tyrannies, most notably Egypt, Saudi Arabia, Jordan, Pakistan, and the Gulf States."* It went on to say, *"Thus, when American public diplomacy talks about bringing democracy to Islamic societies, this is seen as no more than self-serving hypocrisy."*[59]

The social revolutions in Tunisia, Egypt, and throughout the Middle East have exposed both the hypocrisy and failure of U.S. foreign policies in the region. It was "both exhilarating and infuriating to watch the grassroots revolution under way in Egypt," Matthew Rothschild wrote. It was exhilarating "because it proves once again that history is not stagnant." It was infuriating "because the United States has been hopelessly compromised in this situation, just as it has in the face of one revolution after another in the Third World for the last 50 years." Mubarak in Egypt had "brutalized and impoverished his people" but he "served Washington's needs for the past 30 years, and he was happy to cash his almost $2 billion annual bribe that went by the name of U.S. aid."[60] The United States had come to the end of another dead-end road. "The years of Washington calling the shots in the region based on the exigencies of oil, Israel, and a U.S. version of 'stability' are definitely over," Phyllis Bennis wrote. "U.S. empire may be crumbling in the Middle East. The real interests of the people of the United States don't have to."[61]

Our real interests aren't served when our nation's leaders invade and occupy other nations, or when U.S. foreign policies embody double

standards and embrace authoritarian governments. In 1986 an Afghan
fighter funded by the United States told a U.S. reporter: "When we have
driven the Communist imperialists from Afghanistan, we will go on and
drive the American imperialists from Arabia and the rest of the Muslim
world."[62] Bin Laden's grievances against the United States were that "the
US sided with repressive Muslim regimes, killed Iraqis, stationed troops
on holy Muslim soil, and supported Israel against the Palestinians. All
these allegations," Michael Mann noted, "were widely believed, because
they were true."[63] That is why, Esposito writes, many of bin Laden's
criticisms of the United States and the West resonate with the "perceptions and grievances of mainstream as well as extremist Muslims."[64]

RAD recommended putting permanent U.S. bases and soldiers in the
Middle East even though they understood that the ever-expanding U.S.
troop presence fueled anti-Americanism and increased the likelihood of
terrorism. In fact, years before RAD was published Osama bin Laden
justified his call for attacks against Americans saying: the "Arabian
Peninsula has . . . been stormed by . . . crusader armies spreading in it
like locusts, eating its riches and wiping out its plantations."[65] Invading
and occupying Muslim nations in pursuit of oil and influence may make
sense in terms of geopolitical ambitions, interests, and power projection
but increased terror is a predictable consequence.

Responding to the terror attacks with a "war on terror" is itself foolish. The United States experienced a worldwide outpouring of sympathy
following 9/11 but relatively little support for its decision to respond
with war in Afghanistan. It was certainly a sign of the malignancy of
a war culture that the best response to terror our leaders could muster
was a "Pentagon-led war through overwhelming use of military force,
occupation and counterinsurgency, and a CIA-managed secret campaign of spying, harsh interrogation, assassinations, and extraordinary
rendition."[66] Psychologist Robert Jay Lifton writes that "in their mutual
zealotry, Islamist and American leaders seem to act in concert. That is,
each, in its excess, nurtures the apocalypticism of the other, resulting in a

malignant symmetry." In the case of the United States, he says that "our amorphously extreme response feeds a larger dynamic of apocalyptic violence, even as it constructs a twenty-first-century version of American empire."[67]

Michael Mann reports that poll after poll in country after country outside the Muslim world showed that overwhelming majorities "favored extradition and trial" not war in Afghanistan. The "Muslim world was quite hostile."[68] There were many reasons to be skeptical about the wisdom of declaring a "war on terror" but foremost among them is that it was what Osama bin Laden wanted. Nicolas Davies writes:

> In fact, the response of the U.S. government to the terrorist attacks has been exactly as Osama bin Laden and his colleagues intended. They did not expect to defeat the United States by knocking down a few buildings. Nor were they motivated by some irrational hatred of freedom. Rather the attacks were designed to provoke a reaction that would expose the hypocrisy of the United States . . . The explicit goal was to goad the American empire into using its vast arsenal of destructive weapons in ways that would gradually undermine its own economic and military power. Bin Laden and his second-in-command . . . understood so much better than America's deluded leaders that this would be a war the United States could not win.[69]

"Terrorism is not an enemy. It cannot be defeated," retired U.S. General William Odom said. "It is a tactic. It's about as sensible to say we declare war on night attacks and expect we're going to win that war. We're not going to win the war on terrorism."[70] Fighting a war on terror won't reduce terror, but it serves as a useful cover for those engaged in power projection in defense of interests and for a national security establishment that benefits from war, fear, and high military spending. "I'm wondering if our governments don't need this terror—to make us frightened," Robert Fisk writes, "very frightened, to make us obey. . . . And

I'm wondering whether those same governments will ever wake up to the fact that our actions in the Middle East are what is endangering our security."[71]

The conduct of "rogue states," which U.S. leaders find objectionable, is also best understood in the context of U.S. interventionism. The "new imperialism," Mann wrote, "creates more, not fewer, terrorists" and it "creates more determined 'rogue states.'"[72] RAD warned that "adversaries like Iran, Iraq, and North Korea are rushing to develop ballistic missiles and nuclear weapons as a deterrent to American intervention." It then called for regime change in nations that had the audacity to seek a means of self-defense from U.S. aggression. "These are not offensive weapons," Michael Mann wrote, and "they cannot possibly threaten the US." The reason for nuclear weapons proliferation in the global South is because "they produce a big deterrence pay-off at relatively low cost. Above all, they seem to protect a state against American imperialism. The US," he wrote, "will think twice about attacking a country with established nuclear weapons, they reason."[73]

The Korean Committee for Solidarity with World Peoples described what North Korean leaders learned from the U.S. invasion of Iraq. "The Iraqi war taught the lesson that . . . the security of the nation can be protected only when a country has a physical deterrent force." A few weeks before the invasion a North Korean general defended his country's nuclear weapons program: "We see what you are getting ready to do with Iraq. And you are not going to do it to us."[74] Among the many benefits of saying good riddance to empire will be increased security, reduced threats of terror, and greatly enhanced possibilities for nonproliferation.

Restore Democracy and Civil Liberties

An inevitable consequence of empire is serious erosion of democratic rights. Saying good riddance to empire would allow us to restore civil liberties and enhance authentic security. Living in a militarized state has far-reaching consequences. Glenn Greenwald writes:

A country that turns itself into a war-fighting state, a militarized empire, is choosing what kind of country it wants to be. And as long as that continues, everything else—wild expansions of executive power, the explicit rejection of the rule of law for elites, a continuous erosion of civil liberties, ever-expanding secrecy justifications, supreme empowerment of a permanent national security class whose power transcends elections—are all necessary and inevitable by-products.[75]

A militarized state requires secrecy, conformity, impunity, and excessive bureaucracy. Homeland Security has now become a full-fledged subsidiary of the military industrial complex. According to a *Washington Post* series, "Top Secret America," by Dana Priest and William Arkin, at least 263 organizations were created or reorganized in response to 9/11. There are now more than 1,271 government organizations and 1,931 private companies working on programs related to intelligence, counterterrorism, and homeland security in about 10,000 locations. More than 854,000 people have top-secret security clearances, more than 1.5 times the population of Washington, DC. "The top-secret world the government created in response to the terrorist attacks . . . has become so large, so unwieldy, and so secretive that no one knows how much money it costs, how many people it employs, how many programs exist within it or exactly how many agencies do the same work." There is also a good deal of evidence to suggest that this colossus isn't making us safer.[76]

Former CIA analyst Ray McGovern writes that "lawmakers afraid to be seen as laggards in the 'war on terror' threw billions of dollars willy-nilly at a profusion of intelligence and security contractors after 9/11." This is counterproductive and makes us less secure. It complicates efforts "to find a needle in a haystack by piling on more hay," in the words of Julian Sanchez of the Cato Institute.[77] Just as militarism is not defense and undermines authentic security, so too giving up civil liberties does not make us safer. It turns out that restricting civil liberties impedes rather than enhances our ability to detect and deter terror plots. As Representative Rush Holt said in opposition to obliterating Foreign Intelligence Service Act safeguards and to a massive expansion of the government's warrantless eavesdropping power: "It has been demonstrated that when officials must establish before a court that they have reason to intercept communications—that is, that they know what they are doing—we get better intelligence than through indiscriminate collection and fishing expeditions."[78]

Another troubling consequence of the expansive internal security apparatus that accompanies militarism is the criminalization of legitimate dissent. A Justice Department probe found that the FBI during the Bush administrations improperly targeted peace groups and other nonviolent critics of U.S. policies. Just weeks after this report was released the FBI, now under the Obama administration, conducted another series of raids targeting peace groups. Also, a Supreme Court decision in June 2010 on the Humanitarian Law Project said individuals and groups involved in peaceful work to encourage violent groups to end violence and pursue change through lawful means face fifteen year prison sentences.[79]

Following the killing of Osama bin Laden there were spontaneous gatherings of Americans shouting "USA, USA" or singing "We Are the Champions." The president got a temporary bump in the polls, but the euphoria was short lived. Polls consistently showed that Americans were tired of war. Unfortunately, Congress and the White House used the triumphalism of the moment as an occasion to reinforce presidential powers to wage war, extend the Patriot Act, and restrict civil liberties. "Now more than ever, we need access to the crucial authorities in the Patriot Act," Attorney General Eric Holder told the Senate Judiciary Committee. Yale law professor Jack Balkin noted: "We are witnessing the bipartisan normalization and legitimization of a national-surveillance state."[80] As Glenn Greenwald noted, "Even in death bin Laden continues to serve the valuable role of justifying always-increasing curtailments of liberty and expansions of government power."[81]

Saying good riddance to empire is necessary to enhance security and to bring America's senseless wars to an end. It will also allow us to reclaim our democracy and restore civil liberties.

Promote Peace Conversion and Cultures of Peace

We need to challenge the war culture and shift resources, dollars, and talent from war to nonviolence, diplomacy, and to meeting essential needs. This would include taking seriously nonviolent approaches to social change, nonmilitary approaches to security, and the many benefits of peace conversion. If there is one lesson to be learned from the recent revolutions in Tunisia and Egypt it is that they serve as graphic reminders of the power of nonviolence. Nonviolent movements led the successful Indian freedom struggle to end British rule, ended segregation in the United States, overthrew the Marcos dictatorship in the Philippines and communist rule in Poland, helped end apartheid in South Africa, and brought down the Pinochet dictatorship in Chile. Once we challenge the faulty view that militarism and war are effective means to accomplish goals, it opens up space to take seriously the power of active, nonviolent movements and highlights the importance of diplomacy.

Nicholas Kristof writes that "we have a billionaire military and a pauper diplomacy. The U.S. military now has more people in its marching bands than the State Department has in its foreign service—and that's preposterous."[82] War and economic decline are the inevitable consequences of putting your military on steroids while starving diplomacy. "Ironically, nothing undermines American security like the cuts in public spending (infrastructure, schools, libraries, etc.) made necessary by exploding budgets for outmoded weapons," James Carroll writes. "Not guns over mere butter now, but over bread—and books and bridges. This monetary calculus leaves aside the most corrupting dynamic of the war economy, how the nation is driven into unnecessary wars simply by the unleashed momentum of hyper-war-readiness. Over investment in arms leads to their use, period."[83]

So too does over idealization of soldiers. Retired Lieutenant Colonel William J. Astore writes: "The military-industrial complex is a well-oiled, extremely profitable machine and the armed forces, our favorite child, the one we've lavished the most resources and praise upon. It's natural to give your favorite child free rein."[84] "Ever since the events of 9/11, there's been an almost religious veneration of U.S. service members."[85] This idealization of soldiers isn't good for them or the nation. "There is a reverence for the military in the US on a scale rarely seen anywhere else in the west that transcends political affiliation and pervades popular culture," Gary Younge writes. But "while the admiration for those who serve and die may be deep and widespread, interest in what they are doing and why they are doing it is shallow and fleeting." As a result, it is more accurate to say that U.S. troops die because of citizen indifference to their country's foreign policies than it is to say that they die for their country.[86] It is also tragic that idealizing U.S. service members often doesn't translate into soldiers getting the emotional, physical, or economic support they need when they return home deeply scarred by war.

Shifting priorities away from war would allow us to invest in essential services and basic infrastructure that have long been neglected. Let me illustrate potential benefits with four examples. First, one consequence of defining national security almost exclusively in relation to military power has been underinvestment in basic infrastructure for water and sanitation. A *New York Times* analysis of federal data showed that more "than 20 percent of the nation's water treatment systems have violated key provisions of the Safe Drinking Water Act over the last five years." Since 2004, "the water provided to more than 49 million people has contained illegal concentrations of chemicals like arsenic or radioactive substances like uranium, as well as dangerous bacteria often found in sewage."[87] It would take about $17 billion a year to maintain U.S. public drinking water systems. Congress appropriated $1.4 billion. Wastewater treatment systems need about $11.6 billion a year but they received only $2.1 billion for maintenance and upgrades in 2010.[88] It is a curious definition of security that includes funding for senseless wars and production of unnecessary weapons systems but allows millions of citizens to drink unsafe water.

A second benefit of shifting resources away from militarism is that doing so would create far more jobs per billion dollars spent and would allow workers to engage in tasks and production that significantly improve quality of life. One reason a war system is popular is because there are a good deal of jobs and money at stake. Eisenhower understood that part of the allure and the danger of the military industrial complex was that conscious efforts were made to have people in every congressional district in the country beholden in some way to military spending. But military spending is wasteful because it destroys things, produces things with little value to society, and is a poor job creator. Peace conversion offers prospects of millions of additional jobs involving workers in the production or delivery of goods and services that we need. One practical strategy of peace conversion is that soldiers, workers, and factories involved in servicing the war system would transition to servicing peace-time priorities and production. This is important because persistent unemployment is already high and decommissioned soldiers and workers in defense sector industries will need living wage jobs. A report from the Institute for Policy Studies and Women's Action for New Directions describes the good news about jobs if we demilitarize the nation's economy:

> The study focuses on the employment effects of military spending versus alternative domestic spending priorities, in particular investments in clean energy, health care, and education. We show that investments in clean energy, health care and education create a much larger number of jobs across all pay ranges. Channeling funds into clean energy, health care, and education in an effective way will therefore create significantly greater opportunities for decent employment throughout the U.S. economy than spending the same amount of funds with the military.[89]

A third example of the benefits of shifting investments from war to meet vital needs links peace conversion to climate change. During World War II, the United States transformed its economy with stunning speed from a peace to a war economy. The auto industry shifted production from cars to tanks, a sparkplug factory made machine guns, a stove factory produced lifeboats and a merry-go-round production line shifted to making gun mounts. The sale of private autos was banned for nearly three years as the auto industry was ordered to manufacture war materials.[90] We need to muster a similar sense of urgency with a comparable mobilization of resources if we are to prevent global-warming-induced catastrophes. This time our survival depends on *peace conversion*, not mobilization for war. Environmentalist Lester Brown writes: "Assembly-line production of wind turbines at 'wartime speed' would quickly lower urban air pollution, carbon emissions, and the prospect of oil wars."[91]

A fourth benefit of shifting resources, dollars, and talent away from war priorities to meeting essential needs is that doing so could allow the United States to generate an enormous amount of global good will. The world would be a far safer place if poor people throughout the world had hope for a decent future and if we all saw evidence that the earth's eco-systems could be restored. As Nicholas Kristof writes, "education fights extremism far more effectively than bombs. And here's the trade-off: For the cost of one American soldier in Afghanistan for one year, you could build about 20 schools."[92]

With proper values, policies, and sufficient funding, it would be possible to end poverty and restore the health of ecological systems worldwide. Doing so is morally responsible, financially possible, and ecologically prudent but it won't be easy or cheap. It will take "an enormous international effort," Lester Brown writes, and "must be undertaken at wartime speed." He estimates the cost of eradicating poverty and restoring ecological balance to be about $187 billion a year. Brown notes that people may ask if the world can afford these investments but "the more appropriate question is, 'Can the world afford the cost of not making these investments?' "[93] The costs are a fraction of U.S. military spending and could be borne by many nations as part of a global effort to demilitarize. A practical step the United States could take to move this agenda forward would be to announce unilaterally its intention to reduce military spending by 50 percent in five years. This could be followed by an international conference aimed at reducing global military spending and redirecting savings to end poverty, address climate change, build equitable and sustainable economies, and restore the earth's ecosystems.

CONCLUSION

The architects of war and America's grand strategy presume America's moral, economic, and military supremacy, affirm the nation's mission to spread freedom and democracy, and promote U.S. military power as an effective instrument of benevolence and justice. The sheer magnitude of our greatness forces American exceptionalism upon us. As the world's most perfect democracy, we must export it to the world through violence if necessary. It is our duty to act unilaterally to counter evil and defend our interests. To constrain American power by subjecting it to international laws, norms, and treaties (rules to which others are bound) would constrict freedom itself, encourage evil, and embolden adversaries determined to destroy freedom by limiting American power. To criticize America's wars, question motives, examine interests, challenge weapons systems, question military spending levels, or argue against sending U.S. troops to invade and occupy other nations is unpatriotic if not treasonous and reveals an unwillingness to "support our troops."

Methodist Bishop Peter Storey of South Africa, who was Nelson Mandela's chaplain, describes the challenges facing U.S. Christians that can be extended to all citizens:

America's preachers have a task more difficult, perhaps, than those faced by us under South Africa's apartheid, or by Christians under Communism. We had obvious evils to engage; you have to unwrap your culture from years of red, white, and blue myth. You have to expose and confront the great disconnect between the kindness, compassion, and caring of most American people and the ruthless way American power is experienced, directly and indirectly, by the poor of the earth. You have to help good people see how they have let their institutions do their sinning for them. This is not easy among people who really believe that their country does nothing but good. But it is necessary, not only for their future, but for us all. All around the world there are those who believe in the basic goodness of the American people, who agonize with you in your pain, but also long to see your human goodness translated into a different, more compassionate way of relating with the rest of this bleeding planet.[94]

We can no longer be accomplices to war, war preparation, war culture, and seductive mythologies that are reinforced through popular culture, patriotic discourse, and nationalistic celebrations. We can't allow our nation's leaders to spin a version of reality that prevents us from learning from others and blinds us to marvelous possibilities. "Yes, the world can change," Robert Jensen writes, "if the dominant military power in the world, the United States, can change. If the United States could give up the quest to consume a disproportionate share of the world's resources and disavow its reliance on securing that unjust distribution of wealth through the largest and most destructive military in the history of the world, things could change."[95] Militarism is not defense. National security is not measured by the size of military budgets or willingness to wage war. Our appraisal of security must consider defense of borders, environmental sustainability, economic health, and social well-being. Saying good riddance to empire and rejecting national arrogance allow us to embrace the possibility of soft landings and authentic hope. As Jeffrey Sachs writes:

We are squandering trillions of dollars in useless wars, breaking the budget and the national morale in the process. By ending these futile wars and redirecting our energies to the core reasons for conflict—widespread insecurity, extreme poverty, a scramble for resources, and rising environmental stresses—we will enhance our security at a tiny fraction of today's military outlays. By 2015, we should be able to slash the military budget by at least half, from 5 percent of GDP to between 2 and 3 percent of GDP, and redirect a part of those savings to better investments in global stability.[96]

Chapter 6

Values and Vision

To be hopeful in bad times is not just foolishly romantic. It is based on the fact that human history is a history not only of cruelty, but also of compassion, sacrifices, courage and kindness. What we choose to emphasize in this complex history will determine our lives. If we see only the worst, it destroys our capacity to do something. If we remember those times and places—and there are so many—where people have behaved magnificently, this gives us the energy to act, and at least the possibility of sending this spinning top of a world in a different direction. And if we do act, in however small a way, we don't have to wait for some grand utopian future. The future is an infinite succession of presents and to live now as we think human beings should live, in defiance of all that is bad around us, is itself a marvelous victory.

—HOWARD ZINN[1]

INTRODUCTION

We live in difficult times and face critical challenges. Denying this isn't helpful but focusing only on the worst destroys our capacity to do something. Being hopeful in hard times isn't foolish or unrealistic. It is a necessary way of *seeing* the world which allows us to focus on the good as well as the bad in daily life and in human history. It informs and guides our choices about how to live as authentic human beings, to defy that which is bad and tempts us to despair, and to act on our deepest desires for a better world.

Being hopeful in bad times is the essential foundation on which rests realistic opportunities for soft landings and a better world. This capacity is sustained or undermined by the visions and values that guide us. This chapter focuses on values and vision that allow us to sustain hope through creative actions amid serious problems and uncertainties. It describes ways of seeing the world that reinforce transformational values to guide our efforts to embody authentic hope, respond effectively to pressing problems, and build a sustainable future.

WAYS OF SEEING

When I wrote a book about Jesus' confrontation with the oppressive Roman system in first-century Palestine, what struck me most was his way of *seeing* when he looked honestly at his world. He walked hand in hand with the destitute and the marginalized and challenged the system responsible for their poverty. Jesus faced the oppressive world of his time with unblinking honesty because within the parameters of his sight he saw abundant life rooted in the abundance of God's love.[2]

Authentic hope is rooted in the capacity to view or experience injustice without being overwhelmed because we also see existing evidence for and the possibility of greater goodness. This way of seeing allows us to recognize and cultivate hope in ourselves and others. Authentic hope is active and resilient and is guided by vision and values. People who are hopeful in bad times are able to behave magnificently because they hold two important variables in balance. They pay close attention to problems. They allow bad news to penetrate deeply into their hearts, and this changes them. When they look at the world they see problems, but they also see more than problems. People who embody resilient hope, in the words of Meister Eckhart, a thirteenth-century mystic, don't "walk sightless among miracles."[3] They recognize compassion, generosity, beauty, love, sacrifice, determination, and resilience. Amid problems—whether personal, environmental, social, economic, or political—it is important for us to see possibility, signs of hope, and evidence of life-affirming activities pulsating at the heart of daily life. We can recognize that "human history is a history not only of cruelty, but also of compassion." It is this capacity to see and hold on to beauty, compassion, and joy that allows us to act and to live with hope while confronting the problems of the world.

People who embody authentic hope take bad news seriously because it sheds light on something that is wrong, unfair, or unjust. Something needs changing and they are willing to act. They demonstrate that it is possible to learn about or experience injustices in ways that change and lead us to compassionate action. The Buddhist peacemaker Thich Nhat Hanh refers to this way of seeing and experiencing the world as mindfulness. Our "effort is to practice mindfulness in each moment—to know what is going on within and all around us," he writes. "When we are mindful, touching deeply the present moment, we can see and listen deeply and the fruits are always understanding, acceptance, love, and the desire to relieve suffering and bring joy."[4]

Mindfulness allows us to pay close attention to injustice. It triggers within us some combination of compassion for those affected, outrage at the unjust situation, a sense of personal accountability, awareness that alternatives are necessary and possible, and a desire to do something that leads us to act on behalf of greater justice. This is true whether we experience a wrong directly, in which case the injustice hurts us personally, or indirectly, in which case we are witnesses to or complicit in injustices that harm others.

EXPERIENCES CAN CHANGE US

I remember vividly an experience I had as a college student in 1972 that forever altered the course of my life. The U.S. and Indian governments were feuding at the time. As a result, Indian authorities didn't allow our group from St. Olaf College to spend a month in India as planned. We were permitted an overnight stay in Bombay on our way to Sri Lanka. We arrived at night and boarded a rickety schoolbus headed for a downtown hotel. As I peered into the darkness, I saw dozens, hundreds, and eventually thousands of people huddled between the roadways around small fires preparing to sleep outdoors on simple mats of cloth or cardboard. As we entered downtown, it was clear that many, many thousands of people were destitute. I felt like I was driving through the bedrooms of an entire city, only there were no beds or rooms. The oppressive poverty overwhelmed me.

The bus came to an abrupt stop when a religious procession demanded right of way. I looked out the window and within arm's reach was a naked woman dead on the street. Clinging to her was a young child. Her agonizing screams pierced the darkness as my emotional world crashed around me. After what seemed an eternity, the procession passed and the bus sprang forward. A few minutes later we arrived at a luxury hotel in the midst of unimaginable squalor. Rats and roaches scurried about as many dozens of people slept on the ground outside the hotel.

Armed guards ushered us off the bus and into a magnificent hotel. A feast awaited us complete with fine food, exquisite china, an orchestra, and more silverware than I knew what to do with. I was already weak from constant sickness during a month in Ethiopia in which I lost nearly twenty-five pounds. As music played and food was passed around, I felt sick both emotionally and physically. I couldn't eat, and I didn't want to stay in this hotel. I pushed my way past the surprised guards and spent much of the night wandering the streets of Bombay. It was a foolish, dangerous thing to do.

I don't remember everything that happened that night, but I was aware of being changed by what I was seeing, feeling, and experiencing. By the time I returned to take the bus to the airport I had come to a disturbing conclusion: a luxury hotel surrounded by squalor and protected by armed guards was not just a description of my present situation. It was an accurate metaphor for our world. A wealthy minority used real or threatened violence to secure and protect their privileges while poor majorities were trapped outside struggling to survive. I couldn't then know that this insight would lead me to devote most of my adult life to addressing the political, economic, and faith dimensions of hunger, poverty, and militarism. I did know I couldn't survive on the street and that nobody should have to do so. I also knew I didn't want to take my "rightful place" inside the hotel that had been prepared for me since the accident of my birth into a family of relative comfort. I wasn't willing to live in such a world, and I committed myself to try to change it.

I tell this story as an illustration of how paying attention to bad news can open up *possibilities* for personal and social transformation. Exposure to injustice changed the direction of my personal life, my politics, my faith, and my vocational choices. However, this was only one among many possible outcomes, and it is part of a much more complicated story.

HOPEFUL AWARENESS

Paying close attention to serious problems such as war, climate change, poverty, or dysfunctional politics can easily overwhelm us and undermine our capacity for hope. I know from personal experience that awareness devoid of hope is a toxic mix. I set out to change the world following life-changing experiences in inner city Chicago, India, and Ethiopia, and as I wrestled with the implications of U.S. wars raging in Indochina. I had concluded, however, that anyone who laughed or smiled simply wasn't paying attention and so my immediate mission was often to set them straight (I exaggerate only slightly). While doing anti-hunger work through several faith-based agencies, I assaulted people with a constant barrage of depressing facts and figures about the war, hunger, and poverty in an effort to educate and motivate them. I succeeded marvelously in removing smiles and stifling laughter, but I often failed to educate or inspire. Like a spurned prophet, I interpreted rejection as confirmation of my views. The problem wasn't with me, how I communicated my message, or the fact that my absence of hope was clear to anyone but myself. It was that things were worse than I imagined because people didn't care.

Placing too much focus on problems is problematic. This is true for the simple reason that bad news threatens to overwhelm us even under the best of circumstances. Emphasizing bad news can disempower us and others. Cynicism is no more virtuous than embracing or encouraging willful ignorance. If we are aware and engaged rather than overwhelmed we are likely to encourage hope in others. When we are joyful in our work we are less prone to anxiety, fear, displaced anger, resignation, or depression. We open up possibilities for meaningful social changes that depend on many people believing, not only that problems are grave, but that alternatives exist, are worth striving for, and that our actions could make a difference. We are more likely to succeed when we face problems honestly and move forward with a profound sense of possibility. We model hope when we are mindful and refuse to "walk sightless among miracles." When we act on behalf of a better future that we can see, taste, and long for, it empowers us to do something. It also enhances our ability to envision what communities of greater justice might look like and to inspire others to unleash their imaginations and to act. Authentic hope requires that we broaden the horizon of our vision. Illuminating problems can lead to positive engagement to the degree that we shed equal light on alternative possibilities and practical pathways for action.

BAD NEWS

A positive attitude is helpful but it doesn't make problems disappear. The truth is that many Americans have good reason to be anxious. Their own prospects and the country's future look bleak. Each day seems to bring more bad news. The economic crisis has deeper roots than many politicians and pundits admit or understand. Promises of recovery seem empty as Wall Street temporarily rallies while problems on Main Street worsen. An NBC News/*Wall Street Journal* poll from September 2010 showed that 65 percent of respondents thought that America was "in a state of decline."[5]

The bad news doesn't end here. The United States has become a permanent war state, and yet the intolerable human and financial costs of militarism and war are rarely mentioned among the principal causes of U.S. economic and social decline. John Feffer, who co-directs Foreign Policy in Focus at the Institute for Policy Studies, notes that the "gargantuan military budget, even at this time of economic crisis, barely merits a mention in the news."[6] Tom Engelhardt makes a similar point:

> Nor is it just the angry citizens of Massachusetts, or those tea-party organizers, or Republicans stalwarts who hear no clock ticking when it comes to "national security" expenditures, who see no link between our military-industrial outlays, our perpetual wars, and our economic woes. When, for instance, was the last time you saw a bona fide liberal economist/columnist like Paul Krugman include the Pentagon and our wars in the litany of things potentially bringing this country down? Yes, striking percentages of Americans attend a church (temple, mosque) of their choice, but when it comes to American politics and the economy, the U.S. military is our church, "national security" our Bible, and nothing done in the name of either can be wrong.[7]

Climate scientists seem to be fountains of bad news. The pace of global warming is exceeding their worst fears. And despite the fact that human-caused global warming has achieved the status of near consensus among credible scientists, a growing percentage of Americans live in denial and doubt the science, including nearly all Republicans in the U.S. Congress. The U.S. House of Representatives defeated a resolution in 2011 by a vote of 240 to 184 that said simply that "climate change is occurring, is caused largely by human activities, and poses significant risks for public health and welfare."[8] The American Legislative Exchange Council (ALEC), a corporate-funded council that includes ExxonMobil, Peabody Energy, and Koch Industries on its board of directors, has sought to rewrite state laws to undermine efforts to address climate change. ALEC coordinated Republican efforts in numerous states to prevent the Environmental Protection Agency from regulating greenhouse gas emissions. They successfully passed resolutions to impose a two-year moratorium on any new air quality regulations in fourteen states and failed in six others.[9]

These two illustrations of dysfunction make it clear that the hallmark of U.S. politics has little to do with solving pressing problems. Politics is an arena that is often mean-spirited and well funded. As Thomas Friedman noted in a tongue-in-cheek look at how the Chinese might view the midterm November 2010 American elections, "Best we could tell it involved one congressman trying to raise more money than the other (all from businesses they are supposed to be regulating) so he could tell bigger lies on TV more often about the other guy."[10]

A poisonous mix of ignorance cloaked in ideology, anxiety, fear, distorted values, corrosive money power, and corporate influence is turning our political system into a high-stakes mud-slinging match and auction. Journalist Bob Herbert quotes a businessman who captures the essence of the public mood, "I don't know where we are headed but I'll tell you the truth, I don't think it's any place good."[11]

A REVOLUTION IN VALUES

Howard Zinn said in the quotation that opened this chapter that we are to live "now as we think human beings should live, in defiance of all that is bad around us." We are much more likely to do so if we avoid three pitfalls. The first is despair. The cumulative weight of bad news convinces many people that nothing they can do is proportional to the threat and so they do little or nothing. A second pitfall is trying to do too much. In this case cascading bad news is received rightly as a call to action. However, the result of feeling personally responsible for all the world's problems is that we engage in a kind of frantic activism that can be reflexive, destructive, ineffective, or difficult to sustain. A third pitfall is that we fail to see that bad news about the economy, ecology, politics, or war is not just the result of flawed policies (dead-end roads). It is evidence of a deeper crisis of vision and values. This third pitfall requires further explanation.

Given the well-founded dark mood afflicting the nation, it is tempting to always focus our discussions on policies and solutions. We could adopt a medical model to guide our inquiry. Like impatient doctors who have limited time, little appreciation for a patient's history, and few social skills, we could view grave crises as illnesses attacking the body politic. What our sick patient needs is a speedy consult to assess what's wrong (diagnosis), what's likely to happen if untreated (prognosis), and solutions (therapy or some kind of emergency intervention). Using this medical model would seem to make sense because problems *are* grave, bold actions *are* required, and time *is* short. It would also seem to meet the criteria for authentic hope because it would move us into the vital and necessary tasks of critiquing dead-end roads and illuminating alternative pathways.

The problem with a narrow focus on policy solutions is that it bypasses a much-needed and long-overdue conversation about vision and values. Solving problems and achieving soft landings undoubtedly depend on better policies that can only be brought about through committed citizen activism. The problem is that bad policies reflect bad values and better policies are unlikely without better values. The likely result of more activism without better values is that we exhaust ourselves while digging deeper holes. Martin Luther King, a champion of bold action, also understood the need to change values:

I am convinced that if we are to get on the right side of the world revolution, we as a nation must undergo a radical revolution of values. We must rapidly begin the shift from a "thing-oriented" society to a "person-oriented" society. When machines and computers, profit motives and property rights are considered more important than people, the giant triplets of racism, materialism, and militarism are incapable of being conquered.[12]

Grace Lee Boggs, in her ninety-fifth year, including sixty years as a civil rights activist, wrote in 2010 that if Malcolm X or Martin Luther King Jr. were alive today they would want us to stop participating in ineffective protest marches. "Instead," she said, "in every community and city we should be discussing how to make the 'Radical Revolution of Values' not only against Racism but against Materialism and Militarism that Dr. King called for in his 1967 anti–Vietnam war speech."[13] In many ways, the Occupy movements in cities throughout the United States and the world are embodiments of her recommendation and insight.

Soft landings depend on determined actions that lead to profound policy changes. We need to build an ecologically responsible economy that distributes benefits fairly, to reject militarization and war in order to reverse the nation's rapid decline, to consult with the poor and consider the needs of future generations when determining economic policies and social priorities, to take constructive steps to address climate change, and to revitalize a citizen-based politics rooted in hope rather than fear. Given the urgency and magnitude of this agenda, discussing vision and values may seem like a detour that wastes time or takes us off track. It is, however, the heart of the matter.

People's beliefs and actions seem to be influenced more by values and identity than facts. Soft landings depend on millions of people changing their behavior and promoting better public policies. It is unlikely, however, that people will be persuaded to change course by better data alone. When we confront people with inconvenient facts they often respond with greater resistance to change. Ideology trumps facts. We are more likely to have a meaningful discourse if we engage people at the level of their intrinsic values involving family, relationships, friendships, and community.

The problems we encounter on dead-end roads and the dead-end roads themselves reflect distorted values and flawed visions like a mirror. Privileging violence and domination leads to a militarized society prone to war. Emphasizing greed and competition diminishes empathy and encourages inequality. Treating nature as a commodity deepens ecological crises. Elevating the market to a god-like status and placing materialism at the apex of life's purpose naturally unleashes corporate power while diminishing other voices and other values such as compassion, spirituality, and meaning. In each of our communities we need to discuss how to make a radical revolution in values so that we can help this nation gracefully reject the folly of empire, respect ecological limits, and transition to a caring, meaning-based society. Course corrections are possible to the degree that we recognize that the values we choose to emphasize will impact quality of life now and for generations to come.

COMPETING VALUES AND NARRATIVES

"We need now to understand the world we've created," Bill McKibben writes, "and consider—urgently—how to live in it." This will compel us to assess not only what we need but what we need to abandon "so we can protect the core of our societies and civilizations."[14] Determining what we need and what belongs at the core of our societies necessarily involves discussions and decisions concerning values. Competing values and competing narratives vie for our allegiance. Development expert David C. Korten writes:

> The narrative of Empire, which emphasizes the demonstrated human capacity for hatred, exclusion, competition, domination, and violence in pursuit of domination, assumes humans are incapable of responsible self-direction and that social order must be imposed by coercive means. The narrative of Earth Community, which emphasizes caring, compassion, cooperation, partnership, and community in the service of life, assumes a capacity for responsible self-direction and self-organization and thereby the possibility of creating radically democratic organizations and societies. These narratives represent two sides of a psychic tension that resides within each of us. One focuses on that which divides us and leads to fear and

often violent competition. The other focuses on that which unites us and leads to trust and cooperation.[15]

The values and narratives we affirm and those we reject will determine how we understand present difficulties and how we approach the future. If we choose values that encourage us to behave magnificently, then soft landings are possible. If we choose values that divide us from each other and the natural world, then our difficulties will surely multiply.

CRISES AND OPPORTUNITIES

We are faced with two equally valid descriptions of current reality. One describes crisis; the other opportunities. Here are crisis descriptions from ecological expert Lester Brown, businessman Paul Hawken, and farmer-poet Wendell Berry:

Lester Brown: As the world struggles to feed all its people, farmers are facing several trying trends. On the demand side of the food equation are three consumption-boosting trends: population growth, the growing consumption of grain-based animal protein, and, most recently, the massive use of grain to fuel cars. On the supply side, several environmental and resource trends are making it more difficult to expand food production fast enough. Among the ongoing ones are soil erosion, aquifer depletion, crop-shrinking heat waves, melting ice sheets, rising sea level, and the melting of the mountain glaciers that feed major rivers and irrigation systems. In addition, three resource trends are affecting our food supply: loss of cropland to non-farm uses, the diversion of irrigation water to cities, and the coming reduction in oil supplies.[16]

Paul Hawken: Given current corporate practices, not one wildlife reserve, wilderness, or indigenous culture will survive the global market economy. We know that every natural system on the planet is disintegrating. The land, water, air, and sea have been functionally transformed from life-supporting systems into repositories for waste. There is no polite way to say that business is destroying the world. . . . How do we imagine a future when our commercial systems conflict with everything nature teaches us?[17]

Wendell Berry: However destructive may be the policies of government and the methods and products of the corporation, the root of the problem is always to be found in private life. . . . It always leads straight to the question of how we live. The world is being destroyed, no doubt about it—by the greed of the rich and powerful. It is also being destroyed by popular demand.[18]

The problems illuminated in each quote reveal at least part of what we see when we have courage to look at the world with eyes wide open. Destructive corporate practices often backed by popular demand are dead-end roads that lead directly over cliffs that are rapidly approaching. No amount of positive attitude can change the basic facts of our predicament. It is important, however, that our sight extend beyond the horizons of problems to the equally vital realm of countervailing evidence of possibility. And so alongside the above quotes I offer one from Richard Tarnas (founding director of the graduate program in Philosophy, Cosmology, and Consciousness at the California Institute of Integral Studies in San Francisco) and two additional quotes from Paul Hawken:

Richard Tarnas: It is perhaps not too much to say that, in the first decade of the new millennium, humanity has entered into a condition that is in some sense more globally united and interconnected, more sensitized to the experience and suffering of others, in certain respects more spiritually awakened, more conscious of alternative future possibilities and ideals, more capable of collective healing and compassion, and, aided by technological advances in communication media, more able to think, feel, and respond together in a spiritually evolved manner to the world's swiftly changing realities than has ever before been seen.[19]

Paul Hawken: I looked at government records for different countries and . . . I initially estimated a total of 30,000 environmental organizations around the globe; when I added social justice and indigenous peoples' rights organizations, the number exceeded 100,000. I then researched to see if there had ever been any equals to this movement in scale or scope, but I couldn't find anything, past or present. The more I probed, the more I unearthed, and the numbers continued to climb. . . . I soon realized that my initial estimate of 100,000 organizations was off by at least a factor of ten, and I now believe there are over one—and maybe even two—million organizations working toward ecological sustainability and social justice.

Paul Hawken: When asked at colleges if I am pessimistic or optimistic about the future, my answer is always the same: If you look at the science that describes what is happening on earth today and aren't pessimistic, you don't have the correct data. If you meet the people in this unnamed movement and aren't optimistic, you haven't got a heart. What I see are ordinary and some not-so-ordinary individuals willing to confront despair, power, and incalculable odds in an attempt to restore some semblance of grace, justice, and beauty in this world. . . . [We need to pay attention] without apologies of what is going *right* on this planet, narratives of imagination and conviction, not defeatist accounts about the limits. Wrong is an addictive, repetitive story. Right is where the movement is.[20]

Viewed through these lenses it is clear that although the trajectories of present problems are bleak we have immense and unprecedented opportunities to act magnificently and achieve soft landings. Problems are grave, change is happening, and possibilities are immense. Hawken sees so many people worldwide dedicating their lives to transformation and healing the planet that it is nearly impossible not to be hopeful. His hope is active and resilient. Amidst competing evidence, he chooses to live according to narratives of possibility, imagination, and conviction.

Authentic hope requires that we take an honest look at the data and its implications. It may surprise many of us that the data contain not only bleak science but inspiring evidence of human commitment, resiliency, and hope. Seeing this can help us choose hope and join with others to commit our lives to restore the earth, build positive peace, and achieve soft landings.

FINDING OUR WAY, BEHAVING MAGNIFICENTLY

Our task is to embody authentic hope and live authentic lives in a context of declining empire, a warming planet, an economy divorced from equity and ecology, an increasingly dysfunctional political system, and an anxious citizenry. The good news is that there are positive ways forward. Below I offer brief descriptions of important values and goals that guide my approach to solving pressing problems. I do not have in mind a grand vision for our nation or world that could be achieved only by superhumans acting like saints. I am guided by a modest vision in which the United States makes course corrections and becomes a caring society and decent global partner because of the values ordinary citizens choose to emphasize in their personal and public lives.

Gratitude

A good foundation for daily living is to be mindful of the miracle and mystery of life. Our efforts to help our nation transition gracefully from militarized empire to helpful global partner, to address climate change, to build an equitable and ecologically responsible economy, and to revitalize politics will bear greater fruit as we infuse them with a spirit of gratitude. They also will be a lot more fun. It also helps when we are grateful rather than resentful to be alive at a critical juncture in history in which the consequences of our choices are magnified. Jim Hansen, the leading climate scientist at NASA, warns that if "human beings follow a business-as-usual course . . . life will survive, but it will do so on a transformed planet" . . . in a "far more desolate world . . . ," and that "we have at most ten years . . . to alter fundamentally the trajectory of global greenhouse emissions."[21] We can bury our heads or sink into a deep depression or we can receive his words with gratitude as a call to action.

We have choices and our choices really matter. We have an opportunity and an urgent need to decide together who we are as a people and what is important to us. We have an opportunity and an urgent need to determine what characteristics define a good nation, what constitutes authentic security, and what measures indicate a healthy society. We have an opportunity and an urgent need to assess what forms of political participation make sense in our present context. We have an opportunity and an urgent need to wisely set priorities. We have an opportunity and an urgent need to behave magnificently as we courageously confront daunting crises.

Community

There are four dimensions to community that can inform and guide our efforts to address problems and achieve soft landings. First, when we decide to translate our concerns into action we are not alone. When we become active participants in shaping our future instead of spectator citizens, we don't have to reinvent the wheel. We are part of a network of caring, active, organized communities. Our choice to embody hope through creative action connects us to neighbors and to millions of people and many thousands of organizations that are working for greater justice, for peace, and for healing the earth.

Second, one of the greatest unmet needs in our present consumer-driven society is the need to be connected to healthy communities of mutual caring and trust. We pay enormous personal, social, and environmental costs for trying to fulfill this need in counterproductive ways linked to an overtly materialistic culture. Following World War II, retailing analyst Victor Lebow laid out the foundational values of a society driven by market morality divorced from ecological limits or authentic emotional needs:

> Our enormously productive economy . . . demands that we make consumption our way of life, that we convert the buying and use of goods into rituals, that we seek our spiritual satisfaction, our ego satisfaction, in consumption. . . . We need things consumed, burned up, worn out, replaced, and discarded at an ever increasing rate.[22]

We are in the midst of economic, ecological, and geopolitical shifts that require us to change lifestyles, redefine prosperity, reduce consumption, and lessen our ecological footprints as we seek to build sustainable societies. We will need to move away from a throwaway society to one that stresses creativity, durability, diversification, regeneration, proper scale, resiliency, resourcefulness, renovation, maintenance, repair, proper accounting, and adaptation. This transition will be difficult for many people but it presents us with opportunities to make changes that enhance quality of life and build communities of mutual caring. As Alan Durning notes, "we have been fruitlessly attempting to satisfy with material things what are essentially social, psychological, and spiritual needs."[23] Strengthening relational communities will be a principal goal and great benefit to transitioning from a materialistic, thing-oriented society to a meaning-based society.

A third way in which community is an essential value if we are to achieve soft landings is that community can serve as a benchmark to judge the success of our efforts. If we are on the right track then the values, correctives, and policies we promote should enable individuals to be more compassionate and should enhance prospects for healthy, sustainable communities. I like the language that grows out of a variety of religious traditions and secular norms of human rights that emphasize the dignity of each person and our individual and collective responsibility to build caring societies that make dignified living possible. Highly unequal societies with stark divisions between rich and poor make it difficult or impossible for many people to live dignified lives as they struggle with hunger, poverty, inadequate health care, and low self-esteem. "The development of healthy individuals capable of relationships based on mutual caring and service depends on healthy communities that nurture healthful individual developments," David Korten writes. "Healthy individuals and healthy communities go hand in hand, each inseparable from the other."[24]

Finally, as we seek alternatives to present dead-end roads, our understanding and concern for healthy communities must extend from our families to our neighborhoods to the world, from present to future generations, from human beings to all living things, and to the earth itself. Our sense of community must be both intimate and expansive because as problems worsen it is a grave temptation for groups to turn inward, establish rigid boundaries that define insiders and outsiders, and scapegoat others.

EMPATHY, COMPASSION, AND THE GOLDEN RULE

I believe the world would be much safer and healthier if we condensed the essence of all religious teachings and secular norms for justice into these active values: be empathetic; be compassionate; and treat others the way you want to be treated. Empathy requires that we look sympathetically at people and problems and look at solutions through the lens of how real people will be impacted. As George Lakoff writes, "Empathy is a positive deep connection with other people in general and with all living things, the ability to see and feel as they do." He also notes that, "Democracy is based on empathy, on people caring about one another and acting to the very best of their ability on that care, for their families, their communities, their nation, and the world. Government must also care and act on that care."[25]

Compassion flows from empathy like water from a spring. As the great parable of compassion told by Jesus illustrates, we embody compassion when we bind up the wounds of those in need, even our enemies.[26] I've often been asked as a parent what I most want for my children. I know the expected response is to say that I want them to be happy. I've always said, however, that I want my children to be compassionate because I believe they are more likely to be happy if they are compassionate. I also like the language of a politics of compassion. We all have benefited from the individual compassion of others, and we all share in the benefits when our society and institutions manifest caring and compassion and make it easier for individuals to be compassionate.

Treating others the way we want to be treated insures basic fairness and means no double standards for and between individuals and nations. If my kids all like apple pie and I give one a huge slice and the others a forkful, the ones with only a morsel will rightly complain, "That's not fair." When government and corporate leaders collude in promoting policies resulting in most of the nation's income gains from 1980 to the present going to the richest 1 percent we should be astute enough to recognize that these policies don't pass the fairness test. Profound course corrections are needed. Robert Reich says that this absence of fairness reflected in the "increasingly distorted distribution of income" forces us to choose "between deepening discontent (and its ever nastier politics) and fundamental social and economic reform."[27] Soft landings are more likely when we place the value of fairness at the heart of our deliberations about problems and proposed solutions.

Philosopher John Rawls proposes a moral-thought exercise that he believes would encourage empathy in decision making and lead to basic fairness and greater justice, within society. He calls his theory "original position."[28] Rawls says that if we want to know whether a particular law, policy, social structure, or personal action is moral and likely to contribute to greater justice then we should imagine that the decisions we make will impact a society that we are not yet part of but soon will be. The key variable is that when we make decisions about the nature and quality of the society we will live in, we have no idea what our position will be within it. We may be rich or poor, healthy or sick, old or young, black or white, lifetime citizen or recent immigrant, employed or unemployed, gay or straight, educated or uneducated. We don't know. Rawls's moral-thought exercise brings the golden rule into the realm of public policy. If we make decisions about society without knowing our position within it then we are more likely to make decisions that contribute to a caring society that is more equitable, serves the common good, and meets the essential needs of all.

The absence of basic fairness is often accompanied by equally deplorable double standards that cause resentment when practiced by individuals or nations. Do as I say not as I do is a poor ethical code. I shouldn't smoke if I don't want my wife or my children to smoke. I shouldn't drive a Hummer and work for the Sierra Club. My country shouldn't have many thousands of nuclear weapons and develop a new generation of "useable nukes" while threatening to bomb Iran (a country that may or may not be developing a nuclear weapon). My country shouldn't redefine and embrace torture while claiming to champion human rights. Basic humility and respect are necessary correctives to arrogance that leads to conflicts, war, and environmental destruction. Humility and respect require that we listen carefully to others (even our enemies), play fair, live within the framework of established international norms, recognize ecological constraints, see the logs in our own eyes before focusing on the specks in others, and get our own house in order.

CONCLUSION

Values are threads that weave together a broader tapestry of meaning, possibility, and vision. The values we choose to guide us as we seek solutions to pressing problems will likely determine whether or not we find alternative pathways and achieve soft landings. We are much more likely to succeed if we are guided by generosity, not greed, and empowered by a vision of abundant life in a meaning-based society rather than by consumeristic benchmarks and the anxieties of scarcity. It is vital that we choose empathy, compassion, and possibility over fear. There is much to be gained in seeking partnerships, not domination, the common good, not selfishness.

One reason I remain hopeful in the midst of daunting problems is that a basic sense of fairness seems to be hard-wired into many human beings. "Do unto others as . . . " is a near universal value and is recognized easily whenever applied or denied. The impulse to treat others as we want to be treated may have atrophied at present but if nurtured and cultivated in both the realm of personal ethics as well as public policy it still has the capacity to inform, to challenge, and to change us. It's the end of the world as we know it but it's not the end of the world. We are fortunate to be alive at a critical juncture in world history. The values we choose to emphasize in this difficult time will determine the quality of our lives.

Chapter 7

Letters: Year 2055

By what name will our children and our children's children call our time? Will they speak in anger and frustration at the time of the Great Unraveling, when profligate consumption led to an accelerating wave of collapsing environmental systems, violent competition for what remained of the planet's resources, a dramatic dieback of the human population, and a fragmentation of those who remained into warring fiefdoms by ruthless local lords? Or will they look back in joyful celebration on the noble time of the Great Turning, when their forebears turned crisis into opportunity, embraced the higher-order potential of their human nature, learned to live in creative partnership with one another and the living Earth, and brought forth a new era of human possibility?[1]

April 5, 2055

Dear Grandma Hannah,

I hope you are doing well. Mom and Dad tell me they can't keep up with you and that you are in another play next month. I'm sorry I haven't communicated recently, but I've been busy. There's so much to do. I'm in a drama group at the community theater. And it's amazing to participate in the local community-sings and experience quality music pretty much weekly. I can honestly say that I appreciate all the hours I devoted to music growing up. Mom and Dad have been telling me for years that young people like me take way too many things for granted. They have a point, but I am grateful for many things: for music, art and theater; that college is affordable; for the great public transit system that got me here; for good health and that quality health care is available to all; and for our family, friends, and community back home.

I love all my classes. That's one reason I'm writing. I'm taking a history class that is focused on events during the decade of 2012–2022. We're reading a book written by my professor called *The Great Transformation: How People Defied the Odds, Avoided Catastrophe, and Eventually Thrived.* Imagine my surprise when she quoted Great Grandpa Jack in the first chapter. I of course heard a few things growing up about how difficult things were way back when but I thought adults liked to exaggerate. Their stories seemed like scary tales people tell on Halloween. When you hear them you're entertained but not really scared because you know they're not real. Honestly, until this class I had no idea how close we came to permanent energy wars and ecological and social collapse. I'd love to hear your impressions of this time. I'm off to class. I'll write again soon.

Love, Emma

April 6, 2055

Dear Emma,

I get occasional glimpses of your life from your parents, but it's wonderful to hear from you directly. I knew you would love college. You've always been curious, thoughtful, and compassionate, like your mother and father. Those qualities will serve you well throughout life. Your parents are right about how busy I am. I live a full and rich life. I have a small part in a play at the community theater. I still work a few hours a week at the public library as part of a job-share program. My biggest joys are volunteering at the local school and working with the public lands food project. The schools have a student-teacher ratio of no more than ten to one and with volunteers in each classroom the children get a lot of attention and thrive. Music, art, gardening, canning, nonviolent conflict resolution, and meditation are some of the areas where I work with students. My role in the public lands food project is to work with neighborhoods and neighbors to identify, develop, and maintain public spaces where fruit and vegetable crops are planted, harvested, and stored in community "root cellars" or canned in community canning facilities.

Years ago your great grandma Sara was involved in local food issues too. She'd be pleased that local eco-agriculture is so successful today.

You certainly pricked my curiosity with your description of your history class. I will order *The Great Transformation* from the library. I can't wait to read it. I know historians are divided as to which events triggered the great transformation, why we mobilized in the ways we did, and why we had the audacity to believe we could make a difference. I'll be glad to share what I remember about that time and what I think happened and why. Grandpa and I were involved as were many others. It was a scary, delightful time, one of those rare occasions in life that magnify the importance of all decisions.

I'll write again soon.

Love, Grandma

P.S. What quote did your professor use from my father?

April 7, 2055

Dear Grandma,

You probably know that students here and at all tuition-free public universities are required to do "Common Good Community Service." We spend at least six hours a week working with groups or agencies that enrich the life of the community. There are lots of options. I work with neighborhood health teams visiting residents and families to make sure people are well and get attention if needed. Others partner with senior citizens and volunteer at the local schools and libraries. Others work on community art projects and beautifying public parks. My roommate works with an agency that helps people make their homes and apartments as energy efficient as possible, and in many cases, efficient producers of clean energy. You'll be pleased to know that many students volunteer in neighborhood-based public lands food projects like the one you described.

Another component of our community service requires us to devote at least two hours a week to organizing or advocacy. We meet or

communicate with public officials and share our views on public policy
questions that serve the common good. There are also student representatives on the community health committees and the community-business
partnership boards that help guide local business practices. This requirement to be involved in organizing or advocacy was initially controversial
but when it became clear that students were required to be involved but
not told what positions they should advocate for, the controversy died
down.

You asked about quotes my professor used from Great Grandpa Jack.
There were several in the first chapter but two stood out because they
seemed to frame her perspective on the history of the period:

> Authentic hope requires that we broaden the horizon of our
> vision. Illuminating problems can lead to positive engagement
> to the degree that we shed equal light on alternative possibilities
> and practical pathways for action. Hope is more than an idea we
> come to after weighing all the pros and cons. Hope is ultimately a
> choice we make that leads to action. To be authentic, hope must be
> embodied through creative, persistent engagement.

> Imagine what we can accomplish if we stop squandering wealth
> and talents on militarization and counterproductive wars. Schools
> will reduce class sizes and have adequate supplies. Bridges will
> be repaired. The nation will significantly reduce the size of the
> military. Soldiers will be involved in national defense, not power
> projection. Food shelves will be rarely needed. Homelessness
> will be unusual and temporary. Cities and states will have suf-
> ficient resources to provide essential services. More firefight-
> ers, police, and teachers will be hired as the nation invests in the
> authentic security needs of communities and the nation. Critical
> investments will be made in infrastructure and green technolo-
> gies. Public libraries will expand hours and programming. Urban
> and national rail systems will be built. The country will address

climate change. The child poverty rate will plummet. All Americans will have access to quality, affordable health care. This is a fantasy only because we choose to continue on the dead-end road of militarization, which constricts possibilities and stifles hope. It is a realistic possibility once we demilitarize our priorities and refocus governing on serving the common good and refocus our lives on purposeful living.

My professor thinks the Great Transformation was made possible by the convergence of several factors: continuing in the direction the country and world were headed would have been catastrophic; many people recognized that corporate-driven politics was at the heart of the problem and their visions of meaningful alternatives were compelling; and despite reasons for despair enough people chose hope and embodied that hope through sustained action. This led to some major shifts in values, policies, and priorities. I can't wait to hear what you think about all this. I'll write again soon.

Love, Emma

April 9, 2055

Dear Emma,

I agree with your professor about the factors that converged during that important time. I would add that there seems also to have been a good deal of luck involved. I got *The Great Transformation* from the library yesterday and I'm really enjoying it. Scanning the chapter titles suggests your professor has covered the issues and time period well, with one exception I'll discuss another time. I regret that I can't sit down and read the book from beginning to end, but what I've read so far and your letters have already triggered many thoughts and memories, including the time when my dad ran for the U.S. Senate back in 2008. He sought the endorsement of the Democratic Party in Minnesota and did amazingly well. (He lost to Al Franken, who outspent him about twenty to one. Franken eventually defeated the Republican candidate and became senator.)

I like how *The Great Transformation* begins with a description of how bad things were politically at this time and how many signs pointed to 2012–22 being a "lost decade." This is something my father and I talked a lot about. When he was discerning whether to run for Senate, he set up an exploratory committee and website focused on "the most important decade." Dad said that given what climate scientists were telling us and other factors such as war and inequalities, decisions made during the next ten years would likely determine the quality of life for all future generations. And that we had a responsibility to act. I think he came out of nowhere and did well because many people shared his sense of urgency and they trusted him. The focus of the campaign wasn't on him but rather on where the country and world were headed and the responsibility of citizens to envision meaningful alternatives and to act.

Dad also knew that effective responses to problems posed in "the most important decade" required a different kind of politics. (This may have cost him the endorsement because it offended entrenched party leaders who supported Franken, who in many cases had contributed money to their campaigns.) Your Great Grandpa Jack ran as a reluctant Democrat. Dad thought most Republicans were out of touch. They screamed about deficits but supported tax breaks for the wealthy and unlimited defense budgets. They raised fears about big government but supported corporate domination of our political system and all aspects of the national security state. They denied climate change and scoffed at any suggestion of ecological constraints. Republicans said they cared about the unborn but made budget cuts that resulted in millions of additional abortions. They cared more about preventing same-sex marriage than they did about the common good or the health of the earth. Most of all Republicans, seemed to be without compassion or empathy for anyone they defined as outsiders.

Grandpa Jack liked some of the policies promoted by the Green Party, but they were too disorganized to have much of a national impact and thoroughly marginalized within the two-party system. (Remember this was before instant run-off voting and before we shifted to proportional representation that allows smaller parties and common people to have meaningful influence. Back then a vote for a Green Party candidate often bolstered prospects for Republicans.)

My father campaigned all around Minnesota, and he heard the same message over and over from party officials: all the problems of the country were caused by Republicans and President George W. Bush and the solution was to elect more Democrats. Dad would get up every chance he got and say he whole-heartedly agreed that Bush was a terrible president but that all of the bad policies of his administration—war with Iraq, inflated military spending, tax breaks for the wealthy, refusal to address climate change, and many others—were carried out with the complicity or active participation of Democrats. He'd say that we needed a new citizen-based, movement-building politics capable of transforming the nation's priorities by standing up to moneyed interests that dominated both major parties. I'll write more soon.

Love, Grandma

April 9, 2055

Dear Grandma,

I'm fascinated by Great Grandpa Jack's campaign. He must have been very disappointed to come so close but lose.

Love, Emma

April 10, 2055

Dear Emma,

When my father lost it was disappointing but not unexpected. What started out as a long shot almost became a reality. Part of me was almost glad he lost. I wanted him to win because I thought he'd be a great senator and because it would show that a different way of doing politics was still possible and that a truly grassroots candidate can win. But if he'd won I would have rarely seen him and I worried that he'd be beaten down by dysfunctional D.C. politics. Dad saw it differently. He insisted he would have enjoyed being in the U.S. Senate trying to do what was right, saying what needed to be said, and using his office to strengthen the grassroots groups and efforts that he believed were the key to meaningful change.

When he lost he knew he'd gotten his life and family back and joyfully returned to teaching. He wasn't disappointed for himself. He was disappointed for all the incredible people that had galvanized around his campaign, that an opportunity to use political campaigns and politics to strengthen social movements had been lost, and that the pressing issues that led him to run in the first place weren't likely to be addressed.

Dad came away from this experience deeply disturbed by the entrenched interests that dominated U.S. politics. I think it convinced him that only limited changes were possible within the established two-party system and the corporate-constricted democracy. Interestingly, though, he was also surprisingly hopeful. He felt that hope was contagious and that many, many people were eagerly longing to be part of transformational politics. The need for deeper changes became much clearer after Democrats squandered their historic opportunity when Barack Obama was elected president and Democrats gained control of the U.S. House and Senate in 2008. They were elected in the context of deep disillusionment with the direction of the country during the Bush years and on a platform of "hope and change" but under their guidance little of substance actually changed. What concerned my father was that cynicism and reactionary politics would grow out of the failed policies of obstructionist Republicans and corporate-captive Democrats. It seemed likely that the "most important decade" would become a "lost decade" especially after the 2012 election that set all kinds of records for corporate-financed mudslinging and left untouched most pressing issues. His fears were justified but there were some surprises too. It turned out that massive disillusionment with both major parties led to a people's movement to address pressing problems and overturn Supreme Court decisions that affirmed corporate personhood and unlimited corporate spending to influence elections. I'll write more soon.

Love, Grandma

April 11, 2055

Dear Grandma,

I can see why some people thought it would be a lost decade, but it seems like a lot of seeds were planted during the most difficult years of that decade that bore fruit later. What I find interesting is that the kind of political transformation that Great Grandpa Jack modeled in his campaign back in 2008 (but lost) seems to have fully taken root less than ten years later.

Love, Emma

April 12, 2055

Dear Emma,

You're exactly right. It was a discouraging time to be sure, but the work people did during the difficult years laid a foundation for future successes. National politics was adrift and dysfunctional but people engaged locally, regionally, and nationally in remarkable ways.

Love, Grandma

April 13, 2055

Dear Grandma,

I want to ask you about my professor's views on a number of issues, including several events she says were critical in turning away from what appeared to be a lost decade and which paved the way for the Great Transformation.

She describes how Republicans during the first decade of the twenty-first century led the country into multiple crises—fiscal, ecological, social, and international, with involvement from Democrats who nonetheless were big winners in the 2008 elections. The Republicans responded to their electoral drubbing by adopting a strategy to obstruct all reform efforts. The more ineffectual government could be, they reasoned, the better their chances for a political comeback. This turned out to be an effective strategy in the short-term but was harmful to the country, and overall it didn't work out well for them either. Corporations also worked overtime to block meaningful reforms. Assisted by Supreme Court rulings, they influenced elections and flooded Washington with money and lobbyists. Members of both parties continued to support disastrous wars and approve obscene levels of military spending. Democrats offered pre-corporate-approved policies and reforms concerning health care, finance, taxes, and climate change. They were ineffectual and even these minimal proposals were watered down or defeated so that all the major crises deepened.

My professor says the political system was so dysfunctional that it created the conditions for its own demise. Hope to hear from you soon.

Love, Emma

April 15, 2055

Dear Emma,

Your professor's book does a wonderful job covering the "great transformation." There's only one important turning point I think she missed, and I'll write about that later. As for her view that the dysfunctional system led to its own demise, that's certainly true. Many of the progressive changes that took place between 2015 and 2022 were due at least in part to the fact that the existing system had lost almost all legitimacy. It was clearly incapable of addressing the pressing issues at hand, including deepening ecological and economic crises. This led many people to be discouraged, but it prompted others to intensify their organizing efforts, including during the difficult years before 2015.

People in communities all over the country began modeling the kinds of changes that were needed on a national scale. They revitalized local agriculture; retrofitted existing housing for energy efficiency; invested in conservation and renewable energy systems; drove less, walked, biked, and bused more; and worked in a variety of ways to improve public spaces like parks, libraries, and schools. Cities and municipalities throughout the country, adopted instant run-off voting in an effort to revitalize democracy. Many people got involved in working for social change for the first time. The delayed fruit of many of these grassroots efforts was some remarkable changes in national policies and priorities during the latter half of the decade.

By 2015 many states had strong Occupy movements. Most carried out successful "new priorities campaigns" demanding changes in federal budget priorities.[2] People gathered in neighborhoods and communities to discuss problems and possibilities in their communities. A simple resolution was crafted calling for "new priorities" at the federal level. The basic premise was that to improve quality of life and address pressing problems the federal government needed to redirect resources away from military spending to meet essential needs. Although the federal budget technically was distinct from state, county, and city budgets, it was abundantly clear that militarism contributed mightily to state, county and city budget woes. Every citizen and every layer of government and civil society were impacted negatively by war-related priorities.

The fact that resolutions were passed by thousands of different groups in many states served to highlight how out of touch Washington politicians were with the people and problems of the nation. The "new priorities campaigns" helped challenge the war culture, redefine security, and establish a culture of peace. They were instrumental in the huge political shift that occurred during the 2016 elections. Many of the people and groups involved in the "new priorities campaigns" also advocated on behalf of reestablishing a progressive and fair tax system. And these initiatives dovetailed with citizen efforts to strip corporations of so-called personhood rights. These "overrule the court efforts" succeeded in 2015.[3] This forever changed politics in this country and your Great Grandpa Jack couldn't have been happier. It was also 2015 when the Environmental Protection Agency used its authority in a substantive way to impose limits on carbon emissions, which helped address climate change.

In 2016 a new Congress and president were elected to implement policy changes consistent with citizen demands for new priorities. They enacted meaningful campaign finance reforms (from then on elections were financed exclusively with public funds), stripped corporations of "personhood," and overturned Supreme Court rulings that had declared money a form of free speech. They also took steps to address the economic crisis that had continued unabated since 2008. The economy had been crippled by inequalities and rising oil prices, and it was clear that promises that growth would solve the nation's problems were illusionary. Learning from Norway's example, the new Congress enacted a wealth tax to help fund essential programs along with other reforms that reestablished progressivity to the tax system, implemented job-sharing programs to prevent unemployment, and pushed hard to develop renewable energy systems.

In early 2017 the president followed through on a campaign promise and organized an international conference at which the United States committed itself to a 50 percent reduction in military spending over five years and urged other nations to do the same. Others agreed, and deeper cuts followed. At a follow-up conference, nations agreed to shift and share resources and coordinate "peace conversion" efforts. Governments took human, financial, and material resources out of the military sector and used them to create quality-of-life-enhancing jobs, address climate change, end poverty, and facilitate a rapid transition to renewable energy. Many nations set strict limits on carbon emissions, enacted carbon taxes, and took other steps to reduce fossil fuel use. For example, all nations with factories producing automobiles agreed to a three-year moratorium on production. These factories were retrofitted to mass produce windmills, solar panels, efficient rail lines, and other renewable energy systems.

In 2018 the United States implemented a "Medicare for All" health care system that provided universal, affordable health care. That same year Congress passed the "Revitalization of Local Agriculture Act," which encouraged local and regional production, removed subsidies for basic grains and ethanol, and set up mechanisms to spread the model of neighborhood-based public lands food projects that were blossoming in communities throughout the country.

This was a truly exciting time. I hope hearing about this from me has been helpful.

Love, Grandma

April 16, 2055

Dear Grandma,

I can't tell you how exciting it has been to learn about this period. I can only imagine what it was like to live through it and be a part of such profound changes. You mentioned that you liked *The Great Transformation* but felt my professor missed one important turning point. I can't wait to hear more.

Love, Emma.

April 18, 2055

Dear Emma,

I'd like to meet your professor and thank her for her fine work. We'd have so much to talk about. So here is my attempt to clarify my basic agreement with her main points and then add the one I think she neglected. I agree absolutely that politically the darkest days (or years really) were the period of 2012 to 2015. Here we were, living in arguably the most important decade, and yet politically, as one commentator noted at the time, we had "too many five-watt bulbs sitting in one hundred-watt sockets."[4] Many people were discouraged but people didn't stop analyzing, dreaming, envisioning, or acting.

The "new priorities campaigns" challenged the war culture and made connections between distorted national priorities and unrealized local needs. They were also important because they encouraged people to talk about their hopes, fears, and values. These conversations took place in churches, synagogues, and mosques, and in public places such as parks, libraries, and schools all over the country. I think it was within these public forums that we began to re-envision both security and prosperity. We learned to value friendship, family, relationships, and community over resource-depleting consumption. Production became focused on durable, essential goods made largely with recycled materials. We rediscovered the importance of place as jet travel became prohibitively expensive and as we awakened to the richness of art, music, culture, theater, beauty, and the importance of public spaces.

Also, just because the federal government blocked meaningful
changes at the national level, didn't mean that people stopped working.
Much happened during the so-called dark days despite appearances that
we were headed for a lost decade. The local food justice movement took
off all over the country. Nearly everyone planted gardens. The number
of small farms grew and the distance narrowed between where food was
produced and where it was eaten. And some faith communities like ours
were so frustrated that the federal government wouldn't tax carbon that
we mobilized voluntary "gas taxes." We collected and distributed them
to groups working on renewable energy technologies or those engaged
in effective organizing and lobbying. The fact that moneyed interests had
derailed meaningful health care reform nationally didn't stop citizens in
Vermont and Minnesota from passing single-payer systems. These systems worked so well that they became models for the national "Medicare for All" program a few years later. Similarly, people were so sick
of corporations corrupting politics that they mobilized to take back our
democracy, publicly fund elections, and deny corporations rights granted
to real people.

The important event I think your professor missed was the impact of
the earthquake and tsunami that ravaged Japan in 2011. The nuclear crisis that followed certainly exposed the insanity of treating nuclear power
as a viable energy source, but it did more. Before the nuclear crisis nearly
all debates concerning future energy use presumed significant growth in
energy demand and then projected what mix of energy resources could
meet this demand. Most debates or discussions also assumed that future
prosperity would be an extension of the material-based, energy intensive
prosperity many of us had come to see as normal. I think the estimate at
the time was that there would be a growth in energy demand of approximately 57 percent by 2030. It was also estimated that in 2030 nearly
87 percent of the world's energy needs would still be met by nonrenewable fossil fuels—oil, coal, and natural gas. (People who made these
projections would be stunned how wrong they were, how much we have

reduced per capita energy use, how efficient and widespread renewable energy production has become, and how much better quality of life is today as a result of these changes). Of course their demand-and-use projections required a remarkable capacity for denial about climate change and ecological and resource limits. Also lurking behind these projections was the fact that the leaders of individual nations were plotting and strategizing about how they would meet their nation's future energy needs, always presuming their right and need to use more.

In the aftermath of the Japanese nuclear crisis, people began to see that these future energy-growth-and-use scenarios were unrealistic as were present definitions of prosperity. By 2011 it was already clear that the world was approaching peak oil and that production would also peak relatively soon for uranium, coal, natural gas, and other vital resources and minerals. It was also clear to many people that there were already serious consequences to climate change. It was all but certain that war and conflict were likely without profound changes in our approaches to climate change, energy security, and prosperity. Nations that blocked meaningful efforts to address climate change also sought to increase their resource and energy use as overall demand was growing and overall supplies were shrinking. The predictable result was a zero-sum game in which violent conflict was inevitable.

The Japanese nuclear crisis was a wake-up call. Even though it took some time for the implications to sink in, I believe it was a significant factor that led people in the United States to redefine prosperity, focus on renewable energy and essential needs, and enhance quality of life in less materialistic ways. It also pushed the United States to support global efforts to address climate change, reduce military spending, and approach energy security differently.

The post-tsunami crisis discredited nuclear power. It also discredited the belief system that said prosperity was the product of relentless growth that could be projected indefinitely into the future without dire ecological and economic consequences. I think Japan's nuclear crisis led the United States and other energy-hungry nations to abandon the idea that energy security could be achieved through aggressive militarism and geopolitical posturing to access a shrinking base of nonrenewable, climate-changing fossil fuels. This idea had made the world a very dangerous place. Abandoning it allowed the nations of the world to avoid war, support peace conversion, act collectively to build renewable energy systems, address climate change, and redefine prosperity.

Emma, I want to thank you for sharing your class with me, your professor's book, and your own ideas. I'm proud of you.

Love, Grandma

April 20, 2055

Dear Grandma,

I hope you don't mind but I shared parts of your last letter with my professor. She agrees with you wholeheartedly and said she hopes to make some changes for the next edition of her book. She said I should ask if you would be willing to read a new chapter she has in mind based on some of your ideas.

I have one last question for you. You mentioned in one of your early letters that "luck" was one of the factors that made the great transformation possible. What did you mean?

Love, Emma

April 21, 2055

Dear Emma,

Tell your professor I'd be happy to read what she's writing. Reading her book and reliving that time period with you has been very meaningful and has reminded me not to take things for granted!

We were lucky Emma. The climate scientists were clear that our CO_2 emissions threatened to destroy life on earth as we knew it. They understood a good deal but they were honest that there was a lot they didn't know. They worried rightly about tipping points. They couldn't know for sure what the safe level of CO_2 emissions was in the atmosphere or how soon and how deep cuts needed to be to avoid multiple catastrophes. The truth is that for a variety of reasons we got started later than we should have. Corporations spent millions of dollars to create doubt about the science of global warming and to block needed reforms. People died as a result of our delays and our late start could have resulted in a full-scale ecological disaster. I've thought many times during our recent letter exchanges that things could have unfolded very differently. If they had done so, then you might have been writing me from a climate refugee camp demanding to know how I and others in my generation could have ignored the warnings and let a preventable catastrophe happen.

It turned out we did enough and acted in time to avoid the worst aspects of climate change and to lay a foundation for meaningful life for future generations. Maybe that's the most important lesson of all. Those of us who understood the need to make changes didn't sit around debating whether our actions would be too little or too late. We didn't listen to the odds makers. We tried to live our lives with integrity, hoping it was enough, knowing it was the right thing to do, choosing to live with a spirit of hope and joy. I hope you will always do the same.

Love, Grandma Hannah

Notes

Introduction

1. Bill McKibben, *Eaarth: Making Life on a Tough New Planet,* Times Books (New York: Henry Holt, 2010), 2.

2. Lyrics from the song "It's The End of the World as We Know It (And I Feel Fine)," by the rock band R.E.M. first appeared on their 1987 album *Document.* See Wikipedia's description.

3. James Hansen, *The Threat to the Planet* in the *New York Review of Books* 53, no. 12 (July 13, 2006). Hansen works for NASA's Goddard Institute for Space Studies.

4. Benjamin H. Friedman and Christopher Preble, "Budgetary Savings from Military Restraint," Policy Analysis no. 667, September 23, 2010, *www.cato.org/ pub_display.php?pub_id=12151.MM5U.*

Chapter 1: Painful Positives

1. William Neuman and Andrew Pollack, "Farmers Cope with Roundup-Resistant Weeds," *New York Times*, May 3, 2010.

2. Rebecca Solnit, "Hope: The Care and Feeding of," *www.tomdispatch. com*, August 1, 2011.

3. William J. Astore, "Hope and Change Fade, but War Endures," *www.tom-dispatch.com*, July 8, 2010.

Chapter 2: Ecological Economics

1. Janet Redman, "Connecting Extreme Weather Dots across the Map," *OtherWords,* July 18, 2011. Janet Redman is the co-director of the Sustainable Energy and Economy Network at the Institute for Policy Studies.

2. Quoted in Tim Jackson, *Prosperity without Growth: Economics for a Finite Planet* (London: Earthscan, 2009).

3. Ibid., 1–2.

4. Ibid., 3.

5. Statistics on food insecurity and use of emergency food networks are from Children's HealthWatch, *www.childrenshealthwatch.org/page/ResearchFAQs.*

6. Quoted in John Carey, "Storm Warnings: Extreme Weather Is a Product of Climate Change," *Scientific American,* June 28, 2011.

7. Alex Prud'Homme, "Drought: A Creeping Disaster," *New York Times,* July 16, 2011.

8. John Carey, "Our Extreme Future: Predicting and Coping with the Effects of a Changing Climate," *Scientific American,* June 30, 2011.

9. James Hanson et al., "The Case for Young People and Nature: A Path to a Healthy, Natural, Prosperous Future," *www.columbia.edu/~jeh1/mailings/2011/20110505_CaseForYoungPeople.pdf.*

10. Herman E. Daly, *Beyond Growth* (Boston: Beacon Press, 1996), 27.

11. Jackson, *Prosperity without Growth,* 123.

12. Ibid., 187.

13. Herman E. Daly, *Steady State Economics* (Washington, D.C.: Island Press, 1991), 16–17.

14. Ibid., 64.

15. Bill McKibben, *Eaarth: Making a Life on a Tough New Planet* (New York: Times Books, Henry Holt, 2010), 95.

16. Ibid., 47 (emphasis in original).

17. Ibid., 95 (emphasis in original).

18. Daly, *Beyond Growth,* 6.

19. Ibid., 8.

20. McKibben, *Eaarth,* 97.

21. Lester R. Brown, *Plan B 2.0: Rescuing a Planet under Stress and a Civilization in Trouble* (New York: W. W. Norton, 2006), 4–5

22. Barbara Kingsolver in "Water: Our Thirsty World," *National Geographic,* April 2010, 49.

23. Andrew Simms, "We've Gone into the Ecological Red," *The Guardian/UK,* August 23, 2010.

24. Jackson, *Prosperity without Growth,* 88.

25. Ibid., 75 and 77.

26. Daly, *Beyond Growth,* 28.

27. Anne Lutz Fernandez and Catherine Lutz, "Why Do We Worship at the Altar of Technology?" *The Guardian/UK*, August 3, 2010.

28. Joseph Stiglitz, "Gambling with the Planet," *Al Jazeera,* April 7, 2011.

29. See for example, Nick Turse, "Overkill: Future Weapons, Future Wars, and the New Arms Race," *www.tomdispatch.com,* February 1, 2011.

30. Daly, *Beyond Growth,* 17.

31. See for example, Stephen Leahy, "Welcome to Bizarro World," *Inter Press Service,* August 11, 2011. See also a letter written to President Obama by scientific experts opposing construction of a pipeline that would carry Canadian tar sands to U.S. markets, *www.tarsandsaction.org/scientists-keystone-xl-obama/*.

32. "Obama Backs Nuclear Plan," *Minneapolis Star Tribune,* March 17, 2011 (emphasis added).

33. Amory Lovins, "Learning from Japan's Nuclear Disaster," *RMI Outlet,* March 19, 2011.

34. Donna Smith, "Forbes 400 or the Sicko 12," *www.commondreams.org,* March 10, 2011.

35. Daly, *Beyond Growth,* 15.

36. Tom Turnipseed, "War Steals from the Poor and Unemployed," *www.commondreams.org,* September 20, 2010.

37. Jackson, *Prosperity without Growth,* 40 and 125.

38. Vandana Shiva, "Time to End War against the Earth," *The Age* (Australia), November 7, 2010.

39. Lester R. Brown, *Plan B 4.0: Mobilizing to Save Civilization* (New York: W. W. Norton, Earth Policy Institute, 2009), 5.

40. Jackson, *Prosperity without Growth*, 44 and 46.

41. Ibid., 32–33.

42. Antoine Blua, "UN Conference Confronts Dramatic Loss of Biodiversity," *Radio Free Europe,* October 18, 2010.

43. C. J. Vorosmarty, et al., "Global Threats to Human Security and River Biodiversity," *Nature,* September 30, 2010, *www.nature.com/nature/journal/v467/n7315/pdf/nature09440.pdf.*

44. Brown, *Plan B 4.0,* 32.

45. Lester Brown, "Land of Hunger," *Minneapolis Star Tribune,* March 18, 2011.

46. A November 2009 report from the non-partisan Government Accounting Office says: "High-level nuclear waste—one of the nation's most hazardous substances—is accumulating at 80 sites in 35 states. The United States has generated 70,000 metric tons of nuclear waste and is expected to generate 153,000 metric tons by 2055 (*www.gao.gov/products/GAO-10-48*). It takes four to six gallons of water to produce one barrel of tar sands oil, which is four times more water than it takes to produce oil from conventional reserves, according to a 2009 study by Argonne National Laboratory. Meanwhile producing one barrel of shale oil

takes two to three times as much water as conventional oil" (*www.circleofblue.org/ waternews/2010/world/tar-sands-oil-production-is-an-industrial-bonanza-poses-major-water-use-challenges/*). About half the 410 billion gallons of water the U.S. withdraws daily goes to cooling thermoelectric power plants, and most of that goes to cooling coal-burning plants. And solar generating plants using conventional cooling technology use two or three times as much water as coal-fired plants (see Peter Boaz and Matthew O. Berger, "Rising Energy Demand Hits Water Scarcity 'Choke Point,'" *Inter Press Service,* September 23, 2010.)

47. Boaz and Berger, "Rising Energy Demand Hits Water Scarcity 'Choke Point.'"

48. Kingsolver, "Water," 78.

49. Ibid.

50. Thalif Deen, "Summit Failure on Water, Sanitation Would Be Recipe for Disaster," *Inter Press Service,* September 14, 2010.

51. Ibid.

52. *National Geographic,* 44.

53. See *www.350.org.*

54. James Hansen, "Draft Paper: Paleoclimate Implications for Human-Made Climate Change," e-mail sent from James Hansen on January 19, 2011, *www. columbia.edu/~jeh1/mailings/2011/20110118_MilankovicPaper.pdf.*

55. Hansen, "The Threat to the Planet," 3.

56. Searchinger, "How Biofuels Contribute to the Food Crisis."

57. See *www.wgms.ch/mbb/sum09.html* and *www.grid.unep.ch/glaciers/pdfs/ pdfs/5.pdf* for data and analysis.

58. *National Geographic,* 69.

59. Brown, *Plan B 4.0,* 4.

60. Tim Searchinger, "How Biofuels Contribute to the Food Crisis," *Washington Post,* February 11, 2011.

61. Lester Brown, "The New Geopolitics of Food," *Foreign Policy,* May 31, 2011.

62. Michael Parenti, "Soaring Food Prices, Wild Weather, Upheaval, and a Planetful of Trouble: Reading the World in a Loaf of Bread," *www.tomdispatch. com,* July 19, 2011.

63. Searchinger, "How Biofuels Contribute to the Food Crisis."

64. Bryan Walsh, "Why Biofuels Help Push Up World Food Prices," *Time,* February 14, 2011.

65. Carolyn Lochhead, "Dead Zone in Gulf Linked to Ethanol Production," *San Francisco Chronicle,* July 6, 2010.

66. Donald Carr, quoted in "Greenwashing Corn: Industrial Ag Tries to Bolster Its Tarnished Image," *Huffington Post,* June 4, 2010. For the NRI report, see *www.nrcs.usda.gov/technical/NRI/2007/nri07erosion.html.*

67. Ibid.

68. Quoted in Paul Buchheit, "How Wall Street Greed Fueled Egypt's Turmoil," *www.commondreams.org,* February 14, 2011.

69. "World Bank Land Grab Report Comment: Biofuels Cause Land Grabs," press release from Friends of the Earth International, September 8, 2010.

70. John Vidal, "How Food and Water Are Driving a 21st-Century African Land Grab," *The Observer,* March 7, 2010.

71. See *http://nazret.com/blog/index.php/2010/04/24/ethiopia_stop_land_grabbing_now_activist.* Also see *www.farmlandgrab.org.*

72. Josephine Marcotty, "Poison on Tap," *Minneapolis Star Tribune,* February 2, 2011.

73. Anna Lappe, *Diet for a Hot Planet: The Climate Crisis at the End of Your Fork and What You Can Do About It* (New York: Bloomsbury USA, 2010), 7.

74. Food and Drug Administration Department of Health and Human Services, "2009 Summary Report on Antimicrobials Sold or Distributed for Use in U.S. Food-Producing Animals," *www.fda.gov/downloads/ForIndustry/UserFees/AnimalDrugUserFeeActADUFA/UCM231851.pdf.*

75. "New FDA Data Confirm What UCS Has Been Saying for Years: Antimicrobial Use in U.S. Livestock and Poultry Is Massive," Union of Concerned Scientists press release, December 14, 2010.

76. Russell Mokhiber, "Factory Farms Make You Sick. Let Us Count the Ways," *Corporate Crime Reporter*, August 27, 2010.

77. McKibben, *Eaarth,* 48.

78. Brown, *Plan B 2.0,* 4–5

79. Jackson, *Prosperity without Growth,* 45 (emphasis added).

80. Ibid., 32.

81. Daly, *Beyond Growth,* 4.

82. Jackson, *Prosperity without Growth,* 80–81.

83. *National Geographic ,* 48.

84. "Time to End War against the Earth."

85. Daly, *Beyond Growth,* 1.

86. Ibid.

87. Daly *Steady State Economics,* 16–17 (emphasis added).

88. Nicholas D. Kristof, "Our Cowardly Congress," *New York Times,* April 9, 2011.

89. Neal Peirce, "Seven Billion Souls and Counting: the Perils of an Over-populated Planet," *Seattle Times,* July 3, 2011.

90. "The New Green Revolution: How Twenty-First-Century Science Can Feed the World," *Solutions,* August 21, 2011.

91. See *www.transitionnetwork.org/.*

92. "The New Green Revolution."

93. John Vidal and agencies, "UN Warned of Major New Food Crisis at Emergency Meeting in Rome," *The Guardian/UK,* September 24, 2010.

94. "The New Green Revolution."

95. Jim Goodman, "The Food Crisis Is Not about a Shortage of Food," *www. commondreams.org,* September 17, 2010.

96. IAASTD Report. The IAASTD is a joint project involving the World Bank, many UN agencies—the Food and Agriculture Organization (FAO), the United Nations Development Program (UNDP), the United Nations Environmental Program (UNEP), the United Nations Scientific and Cultural Organization (UNESCO), and the World Health Organization (WHO)—as well as representatives from civil society, governments, private sector groups, and scientific organizations around the world. See *www.agassessment.org/index.cfm?Page =FAQs&ItemID=8&pf=1.*

97. Executive Summary of the Synthesis Report of the International Assessment of Agricultural Knowledge, Science and Technology for Development (IAASTD), Agriculture at a Crossroads, 2009. See *www.agassessment.org/reports/ IAASTD/EN/Agriculture%20at%20a%20Crossroads_Synthesis%20Report%20 (English).pdf.*

98. Robert Gottlieb and Anupama Joshi, *Food Justice* (Cambridge, Mass.: MIT Press, 2010), 6.

99. IAASTD Executive Summary, 3.

100. Ibid., 9.

101. Ibid., 8.

102. Ibid., 7.

103. Ibid., 9.

104. Ibid., 4.

105. Ibid., 3.

106. Ibid.

107. Ibid., 4.

108. Ibid., 5.

109. Ibid.

110. Ibid., 6.

111. Ibid., 6 and 7.

112. United Nations General Assembly, "Report Submitted by the Special Rapporteur on the Right to Food, Olivier De Schutter," December 20, 2010.

113. Brown, *Plan B 4.0*, chapters 7 and 8.

114. Antoine Blua, "UN Conference Confronts Dramatic Loss of Biodiversity," *Radio Free Europe*, October 18, 2010.

115. See "ExxonMobil Accused of Funding Propaganda," *Buffalo News*, January 4, 2007.

116. "Climate Change 2007: The Physical Science Basis, Summary for Policymakers, Contribution of Working Group 1 to the Fourth Assessment Report of the Intergovernmental Panel on Climate Change."

117. Ibid.

118. See Mary Milliken, "World has 10-Year Window to Act on Climate Warming—NASA Expert," *Reuters*, September 14, 2006.

119. Hansen, "The Threat to the Planet."

120. "Paul Hawken's Commencement Address to the Class of 2009, University of Portland, May 3, 2009," *www.commondreams.org*, May 23, 2009.

121. Jackson, *Prosperity without Growth*, 35.

122. Ibid., 47.

123. Ibid., 142.

124. Harvey Wasserman, "Why Stewart Brand Is Wrong on Nukes—and Is Losing," *www.commondreams.org*, July 25, 2010.

125. The report is from the IPCC's Working Group Three Mitigation of Climate Change. The full report is available at *http://srren.ipcc-wg3.de/report*. See also Fiona Harvey "Renewable Energy Can Power the World, Says Landmark IPCC Study," *www.guardian.co.uk*, May 9, 2011.

126. Naomi Klein, "Capitalism vs. the Climate," *The Nation*, November 9, 2011.

Chapter 3: Equity, Politics, and the Common Good

1. Herman E. Daly, *Beyond Growth* (Boston: Beacon Press, 1996), 17.

2. T. R. Reid, *The Healing of America* (New York: Penguin Press, 2009), 23 (emphasis added).

3. Richard Wilkinson and Kate Pickett, *The Spirit Level: Why Greater Equality Makes Societies Stronger* (New York: Bloomsbury Press, 2009), 29–30.

4. Robert Reich, *After Shock* (New York: Alfred A. Knopf, 2010), 4. See also Jacob S. Hacker and Paul Pierson, *Winner-Take-All Politics: How Washington Made the Rich Richer—And Turned Its Back on the Middle Class* (New York: Simon & Shuster, 2010), 4.

5. Hacker and Pierson, *Winner-Take-All Politics*, 2–3.

6. Reich, *After Shock*, 6.

7. Hacker and Pierson, *Winner-Take-All Politics*, 3.

8. Ibid., 32.

9. Ibid., 3.

10. Ibid., 22.

11. Ibid., 20 and 25.

12. Reich, *After Shock*, 61–63.

13. Hacker and Pierson, *Winner-Take-All Politics*, 2.

14. See Paul Buchheit, "10 Reasons Not to Tax the Rich. And Why They're All Bad," *www.commondreams.org*, October 20, 2010.

15. Neil deMause, "Who Ate the Dessert?: Deficit Mania Ignores Growth of Income Gap," *Extra,* June 14, 2010.

16. Hacker and Pierson, *Winner-Take-All Politics,* 213–14.

17. Robert Reich, "The Root of Economic Fragility and Political Anger," Talking Points Memo, July 13, 2010.

18. Barbara Ehrenreich, *This Land Is Their Land* (New York: Metropolitan Books, 2008), 96.

19. Reich, *After Shock*, 22–23.

20. Wes Leopold, "Why the Big Lie About the Job Crisis? And the $10 Trillion Answer," *Huffington Post*, September 3, 2010.

21. Adam Liptak, "Justices, 5–4, Reject Corporate Spending Limit," *New York Times,* January 21, 2010.

22. Hacker and Pierson, *Winner-Take-All Politics*, 23.

23. Richard B. Freeman, *America Works: Critical Thoughts on the Exceptional U.S. Labor Market* (New York: Russell Sage Foundation, 2007), 44. Also quoted in Reich, *Winner-Take-All Politics*, 37.

24. Hacker and Pierson, *Winner-Take-All Politics*, 6.

25. Ibid.

26. Ibid., 45 and 7 (emphasis added).

27. Ibid., 43–44 (emphasis in original).

28. Ibid., 249.

29. Ibid., 47.

30. Ibid., 49.

31. Ibid., 47.

32. Ibid., 49.

33. Paul Buchheit, "The Mindless Mantra of Wall Street: The Corporate Tax Rate Is Too High," *www.commondreams.org,* April 8, 2011.

34. Hacker and Pierson, *Winner-Take-All Politics*, 123.

35. Ibid., 114.

36. Ibid., 291.

37. Ibid., 237.

38. Ibid., 270.

39. Ibid., 241.

40. Ibid., 236.

41. Ibid., 212–13.

42. Ibid., 231.

43. Ibid., 211.

44. Ibid., 151.

45. Ibid., 182

46. Ibid., 180.

47. Ibid., 239–40.

48. Ibid., 171.

49. Ibid., 177.

50. Ibid., 195.

51. Ibid., 230.

52. Ibid., 244.

53. Ibid., 245.

54. Ibid., 248. Making a similar point economist Jeffrey Sachs writes that "the only difference between the Republicans and Democrats is that Big Oil owns the Republicans while Wall Street owns the Democrats." See Jeffrey D. Sachs, *The Price of Civilization: Reawakening American Virtue and Prosperity* (New York: Random House, 2011), 8.

55. Hacker and Pierson, *Winner-Take-All Politics,* 245.

56. Ibid., 250.

57. Ibid., 235.

58. Ibid.

59. Ibid., 290.

60. Ibid., 75.

61. Wilkinson and Pickett, *The Spirit Level*, 8.

62. Ibid., 20.

63. Ibid., 19, 25, 26, 39, 44–45, 81.

64. Ibid., 229.

65. Ibid., 23.

66. Ibid., 29.

67. Ibid., 180.

68. Ibid., 173.

69. Ibid., 33 (emphasis in original).

70. Ibid., 11.

71. Ibid., 226.

72. Chris Hellman, "How Safe Are You?" *www.tomdispatch.com,* August 16, 2011.

73. See *http://wealthforcommongood.org/wp-content/uploads/2009/02/Listening-Project-Policy-Doc-2_7_112.pdf.*

74. See Wealth for the Common Good, *http://wealthforcommongood.org/campaign/financial-transaction-tax/.*

75. T. R. Reid, "Myths about Health Care around the World," *Washington Post*, August 23, 2009.

76. Reid, *The Healing of America,* 2 and 3.

77. Ibid.,12.

78. Quoted in Catherine Arnst, "Health Care: Lessons for America," *Business Week*, August 24, 2009.

79. Hacker and Pierson, *Winner-Take-All Politics*, 281.

80. See "Pro-single-payer Doctors: Health Bill Leaves 23 Million Uninsured," March 22, 2010, *www.pnhp.org/news/2010/march/pro-single-payer-doctors-health-bill-leaves-23-million-uninsured.*

81. "If US Is Serious about Debt, There's a Single-Payer Solution," *St. Louis Post-Dispatch,* August 14, 2011.

82. David Korten, *Agenda for a New Economy* (San Francisco: The People-Centered Development Forum, Berrett-Koehler Publishers, 2009), 11.

83. Naomi Klein, "Joining 350.Org: The Next Phase," *www.commondreams.org,* April 7, 2011.

84. Wilkinson and Pickett, *The Spirit Level*, 4.

85. William Alder, "Americans Vastly Underestimate Wealth Inequality, Support 'More Equal Distribution of Wealth': Study," *Huffington Post*, September 24, 2010.

86. Wilkinson and Pickett, *The Spirit Level*, 4.

87. Sachs, *The Price of Civilization,* 179.

88. Wilkinson and Pickett, *The Spirit Level*, xi.

Chapter 4: Good Riddance to Empire, Part I

1. The quotation originates with Benjamin Franklin in a speech to the Continental Convention in 1787. See *http://blog.gaiam.com/quotes/authors/benjamin-franklin/4568*. It was quoted by the Cheney's in their 2003 Christmas card, the Christmas following the U.S. invasion of Iraq. It was passed on to me by former FBI agent Coleen Rowley.

2. Michael Ignatieff, "The Burden," *New York Times Magazine*, January 5, 2003, 22.

3. Harry Kreisler, quoting Chalmers Johnson in an interview, "The Downward Slope of Empire: Talking with Chalmers Johnson," *Counterpunch,* May 7, 2010.

4. See Francis Fukuyama, "The End of History?" *The National Interest* 16 (Summer 1989): 3–18. See also Francis Fukuyama, *The End of History and the Last Man* (New York: Free Press, 1992), xi.

5. "Excerpts from 1992 Draft 'Defense Planning Guidance,'" available at *www.pbs.org/wgbh/pages/frontline/shows/iraq/etc/wolf.html.*

6. Quoted in Andrew Bacevich, *The Limits to Power: The End of American Exceptionalism (*New York: Metropolitan Books, 2008), 112.

7. See *www.snopes.com/quotes/goering.htm.*

8. Bacevich, *The Limits of Power,* 4 and 7.

9. Remarks by President George W. Bush in a commencement address to the U.S. Coast Guard Academy in New London, Connecticut, May 21, 2003.

10. President George W. Bush speaking at the National Cathedral in Washington, D.C., on September 14, 2001.

11. President George W. Bush speaking at West Point on June 1, 2002.

12. President George W. Bush's Remarks to the Nation, September 11, 2002.

13. Bacevich, *The Limits to Power,* 18.

14. Remarks of Senator Barack Obama to the Chicago Council on Global Affairs, April 23, 2007.

15. Karen Tumulty, "American Exceptionalism: An Old Idea and a New Political Battle," *Washington Post,* November 29, 2010.

16. Quoted in Glenn Greenwald, "Obama and American Exceptionalism," *Salon.com,* March 29, 2011.

17. Ibid., emphasis in original.

18. Benjamin R. Barber, *Fear's Empire: War, Terrorism, and Democracy* (New York: W. W. Norton, 2003), 19.

19. William J. Astore, "American Militarism on Steroids," *www.tomdispatch. com,* September 4, 2009.

20. William J. Astore, "'Our American Heroes': Why It's Wrong to Equate Military Service with Heroism," *www.tomdispatch.com,* July 22, 2010.

21. Ibid.

22. See Jack Nelson-Pallmeyer, *School of Assassins: Guns, Greed, and Globalization* (Maryknoll, N.Y.: Orbis Books, 2001). The contras were largely made up of soldiers who had been connected to the U.S.-backed Somoza family dictatorship, which was ousted in a 1979 revolution. The United States trained them in an effort to derail Nicaragua's fledgling revolution.

23. Clyde Prestowitz, *Rogue Nation: American Unilateralism and the Failure of Good Intensions (*New York: Basic Books, 2003), 6.

24. Chalmers Johnson, quoted in *The Downward Slope of Empire.*

25. "The CIA's Intervention in Afghanistan: Interview with Zbigniew Brzezinski, President Jimmy Carter's national security adviser, *Le Nouvel Observateur,* Paris, January 15–21, 1998. Posted at *globalresearch.ca* October 15, 2001. Translated from the French by Bill Blum, *www.globalresearch.ca/articles/ BRZ110A.html.*

26. Robert Scheer, "A 9/11 Reality Check," *TruthDig.com,* September 9, 2009.

27. Bacevich, *The Limits to Power*, 3.

28. Quoted in Claes G. Ryn, *America the Virtuous* (New Brunswick, N.J.: Transaction Publishers, 2003), 196.

29. Emmanuel Todd, *After the Empire: The Breakdown of the American Order* (New York: Columbia University Press, 2002), xvi.

30. Ibid., xxi, 16, 21

31. Ibid., 1, xvii (emphasis added).

32. Ibid.,, 133–34.

33. Quoted in Andrew Bacevich, "Illusions of Victory: How the United States Did Not Reinvent War—But Thought It Did," *www.truthout.org,* August 11, 2008.

34. See Larry DeWitt, "Iraq and Liberal Interventionism in Foreign Policy: Part 1," December 3, 2003, *www.larrydewitt.net/Coloquio/IraqPart1.htm.*

35. Ignatieff, "The Burden, 22.

36. Immanuel Wallerstein, *The Decline of America* (New York: New Press, 2003), 7.

37. Alfred W. McCoy, "4 Scenarios for the Coming Collapse of the American Empire," *www.tomdispatch.com,* December 7, 2010.

38. PNAC was established in 1997 and its website states: "From its inception, the Project has been concerned with the decline in the strength of America's defenses, and in the problems this would create for the exercise of American leadership." Its supporters and signatories to its "Statement of Principles" became a who's who in the administration of George W. Bush, including Paul Wolfowitz, Richard Perle, Donald Rumsfeld, Dick Cheney, Elliott Abrams, Lewis Libby, and John R. Bolton.

39. This and all other quotes in this section are taken from "Rebuilding America's Defenses: Strategy, Forces and Resources for a New Century: A Report of the Project for the New American Century, September 2000," *www. newamericancentury.org*. Italicized phrases indicate emphasis I have added with the exception of their reference to Pax Americana.

40. Michael Klare, "The Coming War with Iraq: Deciphering the Bush Administration's Motives," *Foreign Policy in Focus,* January 16, 2003.

41. See "Nuclear Posture Review," *www.globalsecurity.org/wmd/library/ policy/dod/npr.htm*. See also William Hartung, "Military," in John Feffer, ed., *Power Trip: U.S. Unilateralism and Global Strategy after September 11* (New York: Seven Stories Press, 2003), 67–70.

42. See *www.globalissues.org/article/69/militarization-and-weaponization-of-outer-space* for a description of various UN resolutions on this issue.

43. Wallerstein, *The Decline of America,* 6.

44. Remarks at the Center for Defense Information Board of Directors Dinner, May 12, 2004.

45. "The National Security Strategy of the United States of America," The White House, September 2002, *www.informationclearinghouse.info/article2320.htm*.

46. Ibid.

47. American Service-Members' Protection Act of 2002, Bureau of Political-Military Affairs, July 30, 2003, *www.state.gov.*

48. "U.S.: 'Hague Invasion Act' Becomes Law," *Human Rights News*, August 3, 2002, (emphasis added).

49. Ron Suskind, "Faith, Certainty and the Presidency of George W. Bush," *New York Times Magazine,* October 17, 2004 (emphasis added).

50. Robert Jay Lifton, *Super Power Syndrome: America's Apocalyptic Confrontation with the World (*New York: Thunder's Mouth Press/Nation Books, 2003), 3 and 11.

51. A partial listing of unilateral actions taken and international agreements spurned by the United States, mostly during the Clinton and Bush years, is breathtaking: withdrew from the UN population program (Bush); refused to ratify the Kyoto Protocol to reduce global warming (signed by Clinton, never voted on by the Senate, rejected by Bush), and weakened other international climate agreements (Bush and Obama); refused to ratify the Convention on Biological Diversity (signed by Clinton but never ratified by Congress); refused to ratify the Basel Convention on Transboundary Movements of Hazardous Wastes (signed by Clinton but never ratified by Congress); refused to sign the Convention on the Prohibition of Landmines (Clinton, Bush, and Obama); Refused to support international efforts to curb Illicit Trade in Small Arms and Light Weapons (Bush); undermined the Chemical Weapons Convention by conditioning its signature on crippling exemptions approved by the Congress in 1997, which excluded the United States from most of its provisions; refused to ratify a protocol to strengthen the Biological Weapons Convention of 1972. The United States was the only nation among the 144 parties to the Convention that rejected the protocol (Bush); undermined the Biological and Toxins Weapons Convention (BWC) by resisting a legally binding enforcement mechanism and by seeking to rewrite the Convention to allow the United States to develop and deploy prohibited weapons (Bush); opposed the protocol to strengthen the 1987 Convention against Torture out of fear that it would interfere with interrogation techniques employed at the prison at Guantanamo Bay and elsewhere (Bush); and kept the prison open despite harsh international criticism (Bush and Obama); refused to prosecute Bush administration officials for violating the 1987 Convention Against Torture out of fear that doing so would be politically divisive or weaken presidential powers (Obama); refused to ratify the UN Convention on the Elimination of All Forms of Discrimination Against Women—CEDAW (signed by President Carter but never ratified), and International Convention on the Rights of the Child (never ratified); refused to ratify the Comprehensive Test Ban Treaty that bans all explosive nuclear tests (rejected by Congress in 1999, also opposed by Bush); abrogated the Anti-Ballistic Missile Treaty (ABM), which that restricted deployment of antimissile defense systems (Bush); announced deployment of a National Missile Defense (NMD) system (developed under Clinton, supported by Congress, dramatically accelerated by Bush); rejected the International Criminal Court, which was set up to investigate and prosecute individuals accused of crimes against humanity, genocide, or crimes of war (Bush). For a description of unilateral actions taken, see Clyde Prestowitz, *Rogue Nation: American Unilateralism and the Failure of Good Intentions* (New York: Basic Books, 2003). See also Feffer, *Power Trip.*

52. Glenn Greenwald, "The Looming Political War over Afghanistan," *www.salon.com,* September 3, 2009.

53. Bacevich, *The Limits to Power,* 74–75.

54. Michael Kinsley, "US Is Not Greatest Country Ever," *www.politico.com,* November 3, 2010.

55. Andrew Bacevich, *Washington Rules* (New York: Metropolitan Books, Henry Holt, 2010), 12, 14.

56. Ibid., 13.

57. Ibid., 20.

58. John Buell, Quoted in "Obama and His (Virtual) Virtuous War," *Bangor Daily News,* December 8, 2009.

59. Bacevich, *The Limits of Power,* 171–72.

60. Nick Turse, "A Secret War in 120 Countries: The Pentagon's New Power Elite," *www.tomdispatch.com,* August 4, 2011.

61. "US Drone Strikes May Break International Law: UN," *Agence France-Presse,* October 28, 2009.

62. Tom Engelhardt, quoted in "Terror, American-Style," see *www.tomdispatch.com,* August 15, 2011.

63. Eric Margolis, "Wars Sending US into Ruin," the *Toronto Sun/Canada,* February 7, 2010.

64. Ibid.

65. Quoted in Michael T. Klare and Peter Kornbluth, eds., *Low Intensity Warfare: Counterinsurgency, Proinsurgency, and Antiterrorism in the Eighties* (New York: Pantheon Books, 1988), 48.

66. Bacevich, *The Limits of Power,* 15–66.

67. Ibid., 9.

68. Thomas L. Friedman, *The Lexus and the Olive Tree: Understanding Globalization* (New York: Farrar, Straus and Giroux, 1999), 376, 373.

69. Vandana Shiva, "Time to End War against the Earth," *The Age (Australia),* November 7, 2010.

70. Bacevich, *The Limits to Power,* 58.

71. Ibid., 9.

72. Ibid., 5.

73. Ibid., 168.

74. Barbara Lee, "Time to Repeal Congress' Blank Check on Wars, *San Francisco Chronicle,* September 30, 2010.

75. Medea Benjamin, "With 1000 US Soldiers Dead in Afghanistan, Time to Revive the Anti-War Agenda," *www.commondreams.org,* February 23, 2010.

76. William Astore, "American Militarism on Steroids," *www.tomdispatch.com,* September 4, 2009.

77. Stephen L. Carter, "Man of War," *Newsweek,* January 10 and 17, 2011.

78. Bacevich, *Washington Rules,* 29–30.

79. Bob Woodward, *Obama's Wars,* New York: Simon and Schuster, 2010, 319–20.

80. Bacevich, *Washington Rules,* 134.

81. Ibid., 228.

Chapter 5: Good Riddance to Empire, Part 2

1. Andrew J. Bacevich, *The Limits of Power: The End of American Exceptionalism* (New York: Henry Holt), 168.

2. Immanuel Wallerstein, *The Decline of America* (New York: New Press, 2003), 27.

3. Andrew Bacevich, "Disputations: Root Causes," *New Republic,* October 29, 2009.

4. Martin Luther King Jr., "Beyond Vietnam: A Time to Break Silence," delivered on April 4, 1967, at a meeting of Clergy and Laity Concerned at Riverside Church in New York City.

5. See *www.globalissues.org/issue/73/arms-trade-a-major-cause-of-suffering.*

6. Public Papers of the Presidents, Dwight D. Eisenhower, 1960, 1035–40, *www.h-net.org/~hst306/documents/indust.html.*

7. Frida Berrigan, "America's Global Weapons Monopoly: Don't Call It 'the Global Arms Trade,'" *www.tomdispatch.com,* February 16, 2010.

8. See the National Priorities Project, *http://nationalpriorities.org/.*

9. Nicholas Kristof, "America's Defining Choice: Endless War or Healthcare," *New York Times,* November 12, 2009.

10. Barbara Lee, Time to Repeal Congress's Blank Check on Wars," *San Francisco Chronicle,* September 30, 2010.

11. Joseph E. Stiglitz, "Common Sense, Not Austerity, in 2011," *Project Syndicate,* January 3, 2011.

12. Ibid.

13. Joseph E. Stiglitz, "This Budget Would Never Pass," *Slate,* December 6, 2010 (emphasis added).

14. For see comparative costs of spending for war versus meeting social needs see detailed information available from the National Priorities Project, *http://nationalpriorities.org/.* Use the interactive trade-offs tool. For information

on the citizen initiative, google the new priorities project or contact the author at *jacknelsonpallmeyer@yahoo.com.*

15. National Priorities Project, *http://costofwar.com/en/state/MN/.*

16. Ibid.

17. *http://costofwar.com/media/uploads/publications/whats_at_stake/cow_ whats_at_stake_MN.pdf.*

18. CNN Wire Staff, "Crime-ridden Camden, N.J., Cuts Police Force Nearly in Half," January 18, 2011.

19. National Priorities Project.

20. Tom Engelhardt, "Do You Feel Safer Yet?" *www.tomdispatch.com,* January 22, 2011.

21. Bacevich, *The Limits to Power,* 13.

22. *www.gallup.com/poll/143135/Economy-Jobs-Easily-Top-Problems-Americans-Minds.aspx.*

23. *www.pollingreport.com/afghan.htm.*

24. *www.nytimes.com/2011/01/21/us/politics/21poll.html.*

25. Robert C. Koehler, "Believe in Violence and Be Saved," *www.commondreams.org,* December 23, 2010.

26. Gwynne Dyer, *Future: Tense. The Coming World Order* (Toronto: McClelland & Stewart Ltd., 2004), 9.

27. Eric Margolis, "Wars Sending US into Ruin," *Toronto Sun/Canada,* February 7, 2010

28. EUCOM for Europe and Russia; PACOM for Asia; CENTCOM for the Greater Middle East and a little of North Africa; AFRICOM for most of Africa; NORTHCOM for North America; SOUTHCOM for South America and most of the Caribbean.

29. Tom Engelhardt, "A World Made by War," *www.tomdispatch.com,* October 18, 2010.

30. Mark Thomson, "How to Save a Trillion Dollars," *Time,* April 14, 2011.

31. Ibid.

32. Stockholm International Peace Research Institute, *SIPRI Yearbook 2010* (New York: Oxford University Press, 2010).

33. Andrew Bacevich, "Prisoners of War: Bob Woodward and All the President's Men (2010 Edition)," *www.tomdispatch.com,* September 27, 2010.

34. Quoted in Colman McCarthy, *I'd Rather Teach Peace* (Maryknoll, N.Y.: Orbis Books, 2002), 71.

35. Andrew Bacevich, *Washington Rules* (New York: Metropolitan Books, Henry Holt, 2010), 166.

36. See *http://media.pickensplan.com/presskit/2010/2009_oil.pdf.*

37. Graham Patterson, "Alan Greenspan Claims Iraq War Was Really for Oil," *Sunday Times,* September 16, 2007.

38. Kathy Kelly, "Speaking Truth to Power," *www.commondreams.org,* January 9, 2010.

39. Ray McGovern, "Obama Boxed in by Generals on Afghanistan," *www.commondreams.org,* August 27, 2010.

40. Gopal is interviewed in Robert Greenwald's documentary film *Rethink Afghanistan* as quoted in Jeremy Scahill, "'Rethink Afghanistan' Destroys Failed Logic of War," *Rebel Reports,* December 6, 2009.

41. Bryan Bender, "Taliban Not Main Afghan Enemy: Few Militants Driven by Religion, Report Says," *Boston Globe,* October 9, 2009.

42. Robert Koehler, "Winners Lose," *www.commondreams.org,* September 3, 2009.

43. Ibid., 3.

44. John Foster, "A Pipeline through a Troubled Land: Afghanistan, Canada, and the New Great Energy Game," Canadian Centre for Policy Alternatives, *Foreign Policy Series* 3, no. 1 (June 19, 2008): 2.

45. Ibid.

46. Robert Naiman, "Iraq/Afghanistan: A Promise Kept, a Promise Deferred," *www.commondreams.org,* September 1, 2010.

47. Walter Pincus, "Air Base Expansion Plans Reflect Long-Term Investment in Afghanistan," *Washington Post,* August 23, 2010.

48. Michael Klare, "Two, Three, Many Afghanistans," *The Nation,* April 8, 2010.

49. Joseph Nevins, "Greenwashing the Pentagon," *www.commondreams.org,* June 14, 2010.

50. Christian Parenti, *"Tropic of Chaos: Climate Change and the New Geography of Violence* (New York: Nation Books, 2011), 11, 13.

51. Michael T. Klare, "China, Energy, and Global Power: Twenty-First Century Energy Superpower," *www.tomdispatch.com,* September 20, 2010.

52. Michael Klare, *Rising Powers, Shrinking Planet* (New York: Henry Holt, 2008), 30 (emphasis in original).

53. Klare, "China, Energy, and Global Power (emphasis in original).

54. Michael Mann, *Incoherent Empire* (London: Verso, 2003), 266 (emphasis in original).

55. "Combating Terrorism: Presidential Decision Directive 62," May 22, 1998, *www.nbcindustrygroup.com/0522pres3.htm.*

56. Quoted in Chalmers Johnson, *Blowback: The Costs and Consequences of American Empire* (New York: Metropolitan Books, Henry Holt, 2000), 9.

57. "Statement by the President in His Address to the Nation," September 11, 2001.

58. John L. Esposito, *Unholy War: Terror in the Name of Islam* (New York: Oxford University Press, 2002), 162.

59. Quoted in Ray McGovern, "Answering Helen Thomas on Why They Want to Harm Us," *www.commondreams.org*, January 9, 2010 (emphasis in original).

60. Matthew Rothschild, "Who's Hillary Clinton Kidding on Egypt?" *The Progressive*, January 31, 2010.

61. Phillis Bennis, "Tunisia's Spark and Egypt's Flame: The Middle East Rising," *Foreign Policy in Focus*, February 1, 2011.

62. Eric Margolis, "Old Threat Rings True Today," *Toronto Sun/Canada*, January 10, 2010.

63. Mann, *Incoherent Empire*, 125.

64. Esposito, *Unholy War*, 22.

65. Emergency Net News Service, 1998, *wwww.emergency.com/bladen98.html*.

66. Marwan Bishara, "Neither Wars nor Drones," *Al Jazeera English*, January 1, 2010.

67. Robert Jay Lifton, *Super Power Syndrome: America's Apocalyptic Confrontation with Tte World* (New York: Thunder's Mouth Press/Nation Books, 2003), 10 and 4.

68. Mann, *Incoherent Empire*, 125.

69. Nicolas J .S. Davies "Why Afghans Dig Empire Graveyards," *Consortium News*, November 24, 2009.

70. As quoted in Norman Solomon, "A Speech for Endless War," see *www.commondreams.org*, September 1, 2010.

71. Robert Fisk, "Our Actions in the Middle East Are What Is Endangering Our Security," *The Independent/UK*, November 6, 2010.

72. Mann, *Incoherent Empire*, 15.

73. Ibid., 30.

74. As quoted in Tad Daley, "Taking North Korea at Their Word," *www.commondreams.org*, May 27, 2009.

75. Glenn Greenwald, "The Looming Political War over Afghanistan," *Salon.com*, September 3, 2009.

76. *http://projects.washingtonpost.com/top-secret-america/articles/a-hidden-world-growing-beyond-control/*.

77. Ray McGovern, "For Self-Licking Ice Cream Cone, a Terror Topping," *www.commondreams.org,* July 23, 2010.

78. Quoted in Glenn Greenwald, "The Backfiring of the Surveillance State," *www.salon.com,* January 6, 2010.

79. Fellowship of Reconciliation, "Protect Democracy from FBI Raids on Activist Homes," National September 28, 2010.

80. Quoted in Glenn Greenwald, "The Always-Expanding Bipartisan Surveillance State," *www.salon.com,* May 20, 2011.

81. Quoted in Robert C. Koehler, "Wanted Dead or Alive," *www.commondreams. org,* May 12, 2011.

82. Nicholas D. Kristof, "The Big (Military) Taboo," *New York Times,* December 25, 2010.

83. James Carroll, "Now the Rich Get Richer Quicker," *Boston Globe,* January 3, 2011.

84. William J. Astore, "Hope and Change Fade, but War Endures," see *www. tomdispatch.com*, July 8, 2010.

85. William Astore, "'Our American Heroes': Why It's Wrong to Equate Military Service with Heroism," *www.tomdispatch.com,* July 22, 2010.

86. Gary Younge, "US Troops Die Because of Their Country, Not For It, *The Guardian/UK,* January 31, 2010.

87. Charles Duhigg, "Millions in US Drink Dirty Water, Records Show," *New York Times,* December 8, 2009.

88. Wenonah Hauter, "Reaching the Boiling Point: Our Aging Water Systems Are Long Past Due for a Major Overhaul," *OtherWords,* October 26, 2010.

89. Jennifer Doak, "The Secret about Jobs Military Contractors Don't Want You to Know," *Foreign Policy in Focus,* October 14, 2009.

90. Lester Brown, *Plan B 3.0: Mobilizing to Save Civilization* (New York: W. W. Norton, 2008), 254–55.

91. Ibid., 190.

92. Kristof, "The Big (Military) Taboo.

93. Lester Brown, *Plan B 4: Mobilizing to Save Civilization* (New York: W. W. Norton, 2009), 190, 193, and 215.

94. Quoted in Ray McGovern, "Tortured at the Justice Department? Better Not to Ask," *www.commonddreams.org,* January 25, 2011 (emphasis in original).

95. Robert Jensen, "No Nukes/No Empire: The Abolition of Nuclear Weapons Requires the End of the U.S. Empire," *www.commondreams.org,* June 15, 2010.

96. Jeffrey D. Sachs, *The Price of Civilization: Reawakening American Virtue and Prosperity* (New York, Random House, 2011), 188–89.

Chapter 6: Values and Vision

1. Howard Zinn, "The Optimism of Uncertainty," September 2, 2004, *www.thenation.com/doc/20040920/zinn*.

2. Jack Nelson-Pallmeyer, *Jesus against Christianity: Reclaiming the Missing Jesus* (Harrisburg, Pa.: Trinity Press International, 2001), 278–79.

3. Jack Nelson-Pallmeyer and Bret Hesla, *Worship in the Spirit of Jesus: Theology, Liturgy and Songs without Violence* (Cleveland: Pilgrim Press, 2005), 105.

4. Thich Nhat Hanh, *Living Buddha, Living Christ* (New York: Riverhead Books, 1995), 14.

5. *online.wsj.com/public/resources/documents/WSJNBCPoll09282010.pdf*.

6. John Feffer, "Midterm Miscarriage for Foreign Policy," *Foreign Policy in Focus,* November 3, 2010.

7. Tom Engelhardt, "Our Wars Are Killing Us," *www.tomdispatch.com,* January 27, 2010.

8. Bill McKibben, "A Link between Climate Change and Joplin Tornadoes? Never!" *Washington Post,* May 24, 2011.

9. Jill Richardson, "ALEC Exposed: Warming Up to Climate Change," *PR Watch,* July 27, 2011.

10. Thomas Friedman, "China Is No Doubt Secretly Delighted," *Minneapolis Star Tribune*, December 3, 2010.

11. Bob Herbert, "That Sinking Feeling," *New York Times,* October 18, 2010.

12. Martin Luther King Jr.,"Beyond Vietnam: A Time to Break Silence," Speech delivered at a meeting of Clergy and Laity Concerned at Riverside Church in New York City, April 4, 1967.

13. Grace Lee Boggs, "Living for Change: If Not Now, When?" August 23, 2010, *www.commondreams.org*.

14. Bill McKibben, *Eaarth: Making Life on a Tough New Planet* (New York: Times Books, Henry Holt, 2010), xiv.

15. David C. Korten, *The Great Turning: From Empire to Earth Community* (San Francisco: Berrett-Koehler Publishers, 2006), 33.

16. Lester Brown, *Plan B: 4.0: Mobilizing to Save Civilization,* (New York: Earth Policy Institute and W. W. Norton, 2009), 4–5.

17. Paul Hawken, *The Ecology of Commerce* (New York: Harper Business, 1993), 194.

18. Wendell Berry cited in ibid., 14–15.

19. Richard Tarnis, *Cosmos and Psyche, Intimations of a New World View* (New York: Viking, 2006), 483.

20. Paul Hawken, *Blessed Unrest: How the Largest Movement in the World Came into Being and Why No One Saw It Coming* (New York: Penguin Group, 2007), 2 and 4.

21. These quotes are from James Hansen, "The Threat to the Planet" *New York Review of Books* 53, no. 12 (July 13, 2006). Hansen works for NASA's Goddard Institute for Space Studies.

22. Lester Brown et al., *State of the World 1990* (New York: W. W. Norton, 1990), 190.

23. Alan Durning, *How Much Is Enough?* (New York: W. W. Norton, 1992), 23.

24. Korten, *The Great Turning,* 281.

25. George Lakoff, "Obama's Missing Moral Narrative," *www.commondreams. org,* May 28, 2010.

26. Luke 10:34.

27. Robert Reich, *After Shock* (New York: Alfred A. Knopf, 2010) , 5.

28. John Rawls, *A Theory of Justice* (Cambridge, Mass.: Belknap Press of Harvard University Press, 1971).

Chapter 7: Letters: 2055

1. David C. Korten, *From Empire to Earth Community* (San Francisco: People-Centered Development Forum, Berrett-Koehler Publishers, 2006), 3.

2. For a concrete example of one such actual initiative, see *www.mnasap. org.*

3. For information about actual campaigns to overrule the court and abolish the idea of corporate personhood, see *www.movetoamend.org.*

4. Jim Hightower, "Dim Bulbs in Congress," *OtherWords,* August 23, 2011.

Index

biofuels, 29–31
biotech industry, 3
biotechnology, 43
blowback, 90–91
Boggs, Grace Lee, 160
Bolton, John R., 203n38
Boot, Max, 95
Boucher, Richard, 133
BP oil spill, 18, 22
Brown, Lester, 20, 25, 26–27, 29, 33–34, 46, 146–47, 162
Brzezinski, Zbigniew, 91
Buffett, Warren, 63
Bush, George W., 84, 86, 107, 136–37, 179
Bush administration (George W.), 82, 101, 103, 104, 142, 203n38, 204n51
buy-discard-buy cycle, 22

California, budget deficit in, 124–25
Camden (NJ), budget shortfalls in, 125
Canadian tar sands, 22
capitalism, American, three stages of, 54
Carroll, James, 143
Carter, Jimmy, 99
Carter, Stephen L., 112
Carter Doctrine, 99
Cato Institute, xiii
Central America, U.S. presence in (1980s), 89–90
Cheney, Dick, 82, 203n38
China
    encouraging a cooperative relationship with, 135
    increasing consumption of resources in, 34–35
    water troubles in, 26–27
civil liberties, restoring, 140–43
climate change
    Americans' growing denial of, 157
    creating doubt about, 46–47
    damaging events resulting from, 16–17

impacting water quality, 27–28
linked to peace conversion, 146
as message rather than issue, 50–51
not the primary concern for most Americans, xi–xii
Pentagon recognizing the threats of, 134
responses to, 48–49
treated as military challenge, xiv
climate fascism, 134
climate refugees, 48
Clinton administration, 204n51
CO$_2$
    addressing the problems of, 47
    emissions of, 28
Cold War
    end of, reaction to, 96–97
    victory in, 82
community, as means for addressing problems, 166–68
community-supported agriculture (CSA), 41
compassion, as means for addressing problems, 168–71
Congressional Budget Office, 58
constabulary missions, 100
consumerism, 9
corn, intensive production of, 29–31
corporations
    influencing elections, 181–82
    as threat to society, 79
    using government to rewrite the rules of economics and politics, 62
counterinsurgency, maintaining, in perpetuity, 134
crisis, current reality depicted as, 162–63

Daly, Herman, 19, 20, 21, 22, 24, 35, 37
Davies, Nicolas, 139
Dayton, Mark, 122
dead-end roads, 1, 2–5
decoupling, 21

good and evil, used as frame for global
    conflicts, 86–91
Goodman, Jim, 42
Gopal, Anand, 132
Gottlieb, Robert, 43
grain, increasing demand and prices for,
    29
Grapes of Wrath, The (Steinbeck), 57
gratitude, as means for addressing prob-
    lems, 165–66
Great Game, the, 133
Great Recession, the, 15
Great Revulsion, the, 70
Green Party, 178–79
Greenspan, Alan, 132
Greenwald, Glenn, 87–88, 106, 140–41,
    142
growth
    concept of, trumping the environment,
        equity, and justice, 24
    models, absurdity of, 34–35
    projections of, postponing difficult
        choices, 25
    questioning its linkage with prosper-
        ity, 20
    relentless pursuit of, 19–20
    resulting in ecological stress, 26
Gulf War (1991), 99
Guttmacher Institute, 39

Hacker, Jacob S., 54, 55, 59, 62–70,
    76
Hansen, James, 17–18, 28, 48
Harrington, Michael, 57
Hawken, Paul, 48, 162–65
health care
    militarism trumping, 121
    removing profit motive from, 75–77
Hebert, Bob, 158
Hellman, Chris, 74–75
history, end of, 82
Holder, Eric, 142
Holt, Rush, 142

hope. *See also* authentic hope; inauthentic
    hope
    as choice, 11–12
    cultivating, 152–53
    empowering nature of, 156
    requiring honesty, 11
hopefulness, in hard times, 151–52
Huckabee, Mike, 87
human freedom, perceived limits on,
    25–26
Human Rights Watch, 104
humility, embracing, 127
Hussein, Saddam, 103–4

Ignatieff, Michael, 96
inauthentic hope, 5–6
Incoherent Empire (Mann), 136
income inequalities, 24, 54–55. *See also*
    inequality
India, luxury and poverty in, 153–55
industrial agriculture
    approach of, to animal production,
        32–33
    ecological debts of, 40
    leading to systemic vulnerabilities,
        40
    model of, as dead-end road, 2–4, 32
inequality
    addressing, through promoting equal-
        ity of opportunity, 59
    affecting a larger swath of Americans,
        123
    affecting spending by the rich, 60
    aggravating economic and social
        problems, 59, 61
    defense of, 58
    at destructive levels, 57
    making for bad economics, 61
    politics of, 62–70
    related to health problems and social
        dysfunction, 72–73
    Republican Party as defenders of,
        58–59

McKibben, Bill, 19, 20, 33, 161
medical model, for discussing policies and
    solutions, 159
Mellon, Margaret, 33
Middle East, U.S. military presence in,
    98–100. *See also* Iraq
militarism, xii–xiii, 9–10
    causing dangers for Americans, 136
    destroying the U.S., 115, 119
    dominating U.S. actions and policies,
        106–8
    economic consequences of, 94–96
    increasing Americans' fear, 136
    intensifying existing problems, 119–21
    linked with politics of scarcity, 123,
        124–26
    linked with social decay, 120–21
    not the same as defense, 94
    threatening democracy and defense,
        118–19
    U.S. choosing, over health care, 121
    warnings about, 118–19
militarized state, requirements of, 141
military
    discarding the belief in power and
        usefulness of, 84
    expansion of bases as indicator of U.S.
        intentions, 133–34
    idealization of, 88–89, 114–15, 143–44
    missile defense system, 100–101
    policy of, not intended to keep U.S.
        citizens safe, 84
    U.S., as world's biggest consumer of
        fossil fuels, 134
military-industrial complex, 112–14,
    118–19, 144, 145
military spending
    disconnected from threats or needs,
        130–31
    increase in, 97–98
    reducing, 74–75, 130, 147, 149
    wastefulness of, 145
mindfulness, 153

Minnesota, political and economic climate
    in, 122–23, 124
missile defense system, 100–101
Mubarak, Hosni, 137
Mujahadeen, 90–91
Mullen, Mike, 113

Naiman, Robert, 133
narratives, choosing, 161–62
nationalism, 115
National Priorities Project, 125
National Resources Conservation Service,
    30
national security establishment, sacrific-
    ing national defense in favor of
    projecting global power, 91–92
National Security Strategy of the United
    States (2002), 104
National Wildlife Federation, 30
natural resource management (NRM), 43
nature, response of, to past and present
    growth practices, 33–34
Nelson-Pallmeyer, Jack, running for U.S.
    Senate, 177, 178–80
neoconservatives, influencing U.S. foreign
    policy, 82–83
Nevins, Joseph, 134
new imperialism, 140
9/11. *See* September 11, 2001
nitrogen fertilizer, 30
nonviolence, power of, 143
Nuclear Posture Review (U.S., December
    2001), 101
nuclear power, 23
nuclear waste, 193–94n46
nuclear weapons
    proliferation of, in the global South,
        140
    strategic superiority, 101
Nye, Tim, 108

Obama, Barack, 23, 24, 69–70, 87–88,
    107–8, 112–13, 180

222 Index

taxation, reestablishing a progressive, fair system for, 75
tax code, changes in, 63
Tea Party, 56
technology
    developments in, aggravating environmental problems, 22–23
    false confidence in, 23
    irrational faith in, 6
    keeping society on a dead-end road, 22–23
    salvation through, 21–22
terror
    alternative ways of addressing, 136
    foolish response to, 138–40
terrorism, as logical form of resistance against the U.S., 136–37
Thich Nhat Hanh, 153
Thompson, Mark, 130
350.org, 78
throwaway society, moving away from, 167
Tien, John, 112–13
tipping point, for climate change, 47
Todd, Emmanuel, 94–95, 96, 111
top-secret security clearance, growth of, after 9/11, 141
Transition Town Movement (Transition Initiatives Movements), 41
Trenberth, Kevin, 16
Tunisia, revolution in, 137, 143

unilateralism, 83, 97, 100, 128–29
United Nations Convention on Biological Diversity, 26
United Nations Population Fund, 39
United States. *See also American listings*
    affluent citizens of, insulated from social decline, 59–60
    average hours worked in, 56
    backing oppressive governments in the Middle East, 99
    budget problems of, solutions to, 74

    changing role of, xiii
    citizens needing to reassert control, 126
    citizens not understanding international dislike for the U.S., 90
    claiming moral authority, 86–87
    defense expenditures in, xii–xiii
    Defense Planning Guidance for, written by neoconservatives, 82–83, 97
    economic inequality in, 53–77
    economic problems in, xi–xii
    as empire of consumption, 110
    empire not part of God's plan, 83–84
    ending the addiction to oil, 131–35
    engaged in an arms race with itself, 129
    faring poorly on social indicators, 73
    foreign policy affecting ecology, 110
    foreign policy as expression of domestic dysfunction, 110–11
    foreign policy motivations, Americans having little knowledge of, 89–91
    freeing itself from international constraints, 83–84
    generating good will, 146
    government's role in creating a winner-take-all economy, 62–64
    idealizing the military, 88–89. *See also* military, idealization of
    immorality of, 88
    income inequalities in, 54–55
    increasing its Middle East military presence, 99
    linking ideals of, with military force, 82
    living beyond its means, 110
    living beyond its needs, 109–10
    militarism of, and the economic consequences, 95, 144–45
    militarizing space, 102
    most unequal of the world's developed countries, 53–54